Lesson Plans for the Busy Librarian

# Lesson Plans for the Busy Librarian

## A Standards-Based Approach for the Elementary Library Media Center

**Joyce Keeling**

2002
LIBRARIES UNLIMITED
A Division of Greenwood Publishing Group, Inc.
Greenwood Village, Colorado

Libraries Unlimited
A Division of Greenwood Publishing Group, Inc.
7730 East Belleview Avenue
Suite A200
Greenwood Village, CO 80111
1-800-237-6124
www.lu.com

**Library of Congress Cataloging-in-Publication Data**

Keeling, Joyce.
    Lesson plans for the busy librarian : a standards-based approach for the elementary library media center / Joyce Keeling.
        p. cm.
    Includes bibliographical references and index.
    ISBN 1-56308-869-X
    1. Library orientation for school children--United States.  2. Information literacy--Study and teaching (Elementary)--United States.  3. Elementary school libraries--Activity programs--United States.  4. Media programs (Education)--United States  I. Title.

Z711.2 .K36 2002
027.62'5--dc21                                                                                    2001054379

# Dedication

Thanks go to Nova software for use of their clip art, *Art Explosion 125,000 Images*, and to the publishers of the suggested resources included in this book.

A special thanks goes to my husband, Verlyn, and all of my family for their months of support.

# Contents

# Introduction

As the old saying goes, it takes a special person to be a teacher. I believe that it takes a caring person to teach essential library skills with a busy teaching schedule. Moreover, avenues of enriched informational-based learning occur if we apply professional standards. In order to address the needs for students' information literacy, this book provides quick and easy library lessons for kindergarten through fifth-grade students based on educational standards.

Information literacy can be defined as the acquisition of library skills and literature appreciation. Simply stated, the foundation of teaching library skills or information literacy is to teach students how to find something, use it, and put it to good use. Information literacy is based on the mission of the school library media program, which is to provide intellectual and physical access and instruction while using all formats of materials (e.g., books, CD-ROMs, videos, and other resources). Working toward this goal encourages student competence and interest in reading, viewing, and using information.

In teaching information literacy, the library media specialist considers the learning skills and abilities of all students while working collaboratively with other teachers. Information literacy involves students using their critical thinking, decision-making, and problem-solving skills toward the unified goal of global information acquisition. Library information skills and literary appreciation can merge with content curriculum in all kindergarten through fifth-grade classes. Here it evolves into a unique blending among all teachers teaming up with the library media specialist to bring information and literary appreciation into each and every elementary classroom. Team effort provides the pathway to a learning-rich informational environment, where individualized learning needs are fulfilled.

A combined effort of information literacy is needed in order to give students the skills to gather and process materials for lifelong learning. Information literacy is also needed for students to become active participants of information from their present to their future global communities as information changes. Moreover, active, individualized learning is seen through all teachers' use of different learning and teaching methods, as teachers reach out to different ways of student learning. Gardner created seven methods for teachers to reach all student-learning styles.

Gardner's (1983) multiple intelligences are as follows:

1. The mathematical learner enjoys the challenges of math problems, computers, thinking logically, experimenting, and playing challenging strategic games.

2. The linguistic learner likes to write, tell stories, read, spell, and do crossword puzzles. He or she has a good memory for names, places, dates, or trivia.

3. The spatial learner likes to imagine, to daydream, to do jigsaw puzzles, to create with art and to draw, and enjoys movies or visuals. He or she also easily reads maps and charts and thinks visually.

4. The musical learner translates language into rhythm. He or she enjoys playing music and singing and listening to music while studying.

5. The bodily kinesthetic learner does well in sports, physical activities, and crafts such as woodworking or sewing and enjoys acting. He or she needs to move, to be active, and to use the body for learning.

Gardner puts learners into two additional categories: Intrapersonal learners may prefer to reflect on how they learn and act individually. Interpersonal learners may be good at bringing about group goals.

Another important aspect in the instruction of school library skills is the use of professional and educational standards to ensure that all students have the opportunity to become skilled at information access. Standards, such as those found in the American Association of School Librarians and Association for Educational Communications and Technology (AASL/AECT), ensure that all students will have the chance to become effective contributors to their ever-changing world of print and technological information formats. The AASL/AECT standards also guarantee that all students are independently literate in the use of all forms of information in their society. Following is a list of these standards.

# Information Literacy Standards (AASL/AECT)*

1. Students who are information literate access information efficiently and effectively.

2. Students who are information literate evaluate information critically and competently.

3. Students who are information literate use information accurately and creatively.

4. Students who are independent learners are information literate and pursue information related to personal interests.

5. Students who are independent learners are information literate and appreciate literature and other creative expressions of information.

6. Students who are independent learners are information literate and strive for excellence in information seeking knowledge generation.

7. Students who contribute positively to the learning community and to society are information literate and recognize the importance of information to a democratic society.

8. Students who contribute positively to the learning community and to society are information literate and practice ethical behavior in regard to information and information technology.

9. Students who contribute positively to the learning community and to society are information literate and participate effectively in groups to pursue and generate information.

*From *Information Power: Building Partnerships for Learning* by American Association of School Librarians and Association for Educational Communications and Technology. Copyright © 1998 American Library Association and Association for Educational Communications and Technology. Reprinted by permission of the American Library Association.

Teachers and library media specialists can also find professional and educational library standards within the language arts areas of Kendall and Marzano's National Standards and Benchmarks of the Mid-continent Research for Education and Learning (McREL). These language arts standards strive for student competency in many areas, including information literacy and literary appreciation. McREL standards specifically geared to specific grade levels are included in each chapter. Applications of both AASL/AECT and the McREL standards will be seen as goals and reflected in objectives that will ensure observed student growth, as well as the growth of the library program. Thus, these national standards provide a critical foundation for information-based learning across the school curriculum. Consequently, information literacy standards address the ongoing needs of all students as they are observed in their acquisition of information-empowered literacy.

This book employs Gardner's original learning styles to further the developmental information literacy of all kindergarten through fifth-grade students. It will provide a solid base of library lessons based on the AASL/AECT standards along with the McREL or Kendall and Marzano National Information Literacy Standards and Benchmarks, which serves as library lesson goals. Objectives are reflected from these standards for all lessons, creating the necessary balance for professionally taught lessons. The lessons provide quick-and-easy, twenty-minute lessons for all teacher teams who seek to provide standards-based library lessons. Library lessons should be appealing and yet be a valuable learning tool. I use these tried-and-true lessons in my library classrooms, and they do reveal observable, positive, long-term, information-literate students.

These lessons can be modified to fit the individualized needs of teachers and students. Moreover, they can be used for library classroom discussions or for student worksheets. I hope that busy librarians or teachers of library skills, striving to meet all the needs of all students, will find the lessons useful in a busy world. Students need carefully planned opportunities to learn how to access and use information and literature. Students are part of an information-rich world of learning, where the ability to access and process information—and to use that information competently—is a necessary part of lifelong independent learning.

As a teaching team leader, it is up to the school library media specialist or the library teacher to develop library lessons steeped in national standards and then sweetened according to different learning styles to ensure student success. Students must be able to access information and appreciate literature effectively, accurately, and creatively for their own enjoyment today and to become effective members of their learning communities in the future.

Information literacy or the ability to use and access information in an information-rich world of print and technological formats will indeed be met for all elementary students through standards-based lessons. These library lessons will provide students the skills to listen, view, and use information in their library—and throughout global classrooms as the world of information changes and challenges them. These standards-based lessons will strengthen the entire school program to ensure that information literacy will be heard across the entire curriculum and echoed throughout a student's lifetime of learning.

**Enjoy!**

Joyce Van Raden Keeling
Library Media Specialist

# Chapter 1

## Kindergarten Lesson Plans

In order to create solid professional-based library lesson plans, the following selected Kendall and Marzano or McREL National Education Standards and Benchmarks for Kindergarten were chosen from the area of language arts, as it directly correlates with library information and appreciation skills. Furthermore, the AASL (American Association of School Libraries) and the AECT (Association for Educational Communications and Technology) list of Information Literacy Standards were applied to every lesson to ensure that all students will develop literary appreciation and will be effective users of information and ideas (listed in the Introduction). Teaching objectives were also given for each lesson as linked to the standards or active goals. Finally, Gardner's multiple intelligences are also integrated into each lesson, as all students have different methods of learning (also listed in the Introduction).

*Each lesson plan has a direct reference to the following numbered McREL benchmarks under the corresponding standards, as well as a direct reference to AASL/AECT standards.* Finally, all of the following twenty-minute lesson plans should be used in conjunction with the other teachers whenever possible. Moreover, all lesson plans are not the only means, but some of many, for library instruction. The following lessons can provide whole group discussion ideas, or they can provide individual or small group worksheet work.

# Kindergarten Library Standards and Language Arts Benchmarks (McREL)*

Kindergarten students will be able to

- Demonstrate competence in the general skills and strategies of the reading process (Standard 5)

    1. Understand that reading is a way of gaining information about the world

    2. Use picture clues and picture captions as an aid to comprehension

- Demonstrate competence in general skills and strategies for reading literature (Standard 6)

    3. Comprehend the basic plot of simple stories

    4. Make simple inferences regarding "what will happen next" or "how things could have turned out differently"

- Demonstrate a familiarity with selected literary works of enduring quality (Standard 13)

    5. When prompted by the teacher, recite the texts of a variety of familiar rhymes

    6. Demonstrate knowledge of the plots and major characters of selected classic fairy tales, folktales, legends, and fables from around the world

    7. Demonstrate a basic familiarity with selected fiction and poetry

    8. Demonstrate a basic familiarity with selected works of nonfiction

# Putting a Finger on Dinosaurs

## Standards

Students will

- Demonstrate familiarity with selected works of fiction and poetry (McREL 7)
- Appreciate literature and other creative expressions (AASL/AECT 5)

## Objectives

After listening to a fictional dinosaurs book, students will analyze it to determine what parts made it imaginary. Students create finger puppets and then act out a story with them.

## Directions

1. The art or library teacher makes student copies of the dinosaur puppet included here. The art teacher may direct the dinosaur puppet activity with the help of the library teacher.

2. The library teacher reads a fictional story about dinosaurs (such as *Patrick's Dinosaurs* by Carol Carrick or *The Berenstain Bears and the Dinosaurs* by Stan and Jan Berenstain).

3. Students discuss which parts of the story make it fiction.

4. Students color and cut out dinosaur finger puppets as directed by the art or library teacher.

5. The strips for the finger puppets are given below the dinosaur. The strips should be taped to fit around the student's fingers. The dinosaurs will be taped on the finger strips.

6. Students act out portions of the dinosaur book using their finger puppets.

7. The science teacher may use this lesson as a preview for the dinosaur science unit.

## Learning Styles

Spatial (coloring), intrapersonal (working alone), and bodily kinesthetic (acting)

## Teaching Team

Art, library, and science teachers

## Suggested Resources

Berenstain, Stan, and Jan Berenstain. *The Berenstain Bears and the Dinosaurs*. New York: Random House, 1984.

Carrick, Carol. Illustrated by Donald Carrick. *Patrick's Dinosaurs*. New York: Houghton Mifflin, 1983.

**Teddy Bear**

Where will you go, Teddy Bear?
Out of the window? Do beware!
Where will you go, Teddy Bear?
Come home safely, to my chair.
by Hinderene Van Raden

## Standards

Students will

- Comprehend the basic plot of simple stories (McREL 3)
- Demonstrate a basic familiarity with selected fiction and poetry (McREL 7)
- Appreciate literature and other creative expressions (AASL/AECT 5)
- Practice ethical behavior in regard to information and information technology (AASL/AECT 8)

## Objectives

Students compare the plots of two fictional books about teddy bears. Students realize that poems have rhyming lines by repeating and discussing a teddy bear rhyming poem. Students color and cut out teddy bear finger puppets.

## Directions

1.  The bear worksheets included here should be copied on heavier paper for finger puppets.
2.  The library teacher reads two teddy bear fiction books. (Suggested titles are *Humphrey's Bear* by Jan Wahl or *Sleep Well, Little Bear* by Quint Buchholz.)
3.  Students discuss the main plot or what happened to the teddy bear in each book. They should also discuss the kind of adventures the bear had.
4.  Because kindergarten students enjoy reciting poems or rhymes, the worksheet has a rhyme or poem that refers to the adventures of teddy bears from the suggested book titles.
5.  After the teacher reminds students to be cautious using scissors and other art tools, students color and cut out the teddy bear finger puppets as directed by the art or library teacher. The students can make the finger puppets in art class.
6.  If desired, the language arts teacher can have students act out plays with their puppets in English class. Students can act out the book's plot or move their puppets with the rhythm of the rhyme as they repeat it.
7.  As a follow-up, students can run the CD-ROM *Bear Family Adventure*.

## Learning Styles

Linguistic (discussing the books), bodily kinesthetic (acting), spatial (imagining), and musical (repeating the rhythm of poetry)

## Teaching Team

Art, language arts, and library teachers

## Suggested Resources

*Bear Family Adventure*. Cambridge, MA: Learning Company, 2000 [CD-ROM].

Buchholz, Quint. *Sleep Well, Little Bear*. New York: Farrar, Straus & Giroux, 1994.

Mangan, Anne. *Little Teddy Left Behind*. Stamford, CT: Long Meadow Press, 1995.

Wahl, Jan. *Humphrey's Bear*. New York: Henry Holt, 1987.

# Busy, Buzzing Bees

## Standards

Students will

- Understand that reading is a way of gaining information about the world (McREL 1)
- Demonstrate a basic familiarity with selected works of nonfiction (McREL 8)
- Access information efficiently and effectively (AASL/AECT 1)
- Evaluate information critically and competently (AASL/AECT 2)
- Participate effectively in groups to pursue and use information (AASL/AECT 9)

## Objectives

Students acquire simple facts about bees from nonfiction books after hearing and discussing parts of those books. Students create a bee mobile by coloring the bee worksheets and by attaching the bees to the hives.

## Directions

1. The library teacher reads four or five facts about bees from some easy-reading nonfiction books (such as *Discovering Bees and Wasps* by Christopher O'Toole or *The Honey Makers* by Gail Gibbons).
2. The teacher shows students pictures in the books and then has the class explain them.
3. The teacher asks students what they learned about bees.
4. Students color the hive and the bees on the two bee worksheets. They will make bee mobiles from the worksheets.
5. Students can make the bee mobile in art class by attaching the two bee strips to the hive. Students may want to use yellow yarn or ribbon to hang their mobiles.
6. The bee mobiles can be hung in the classroom or library media center.
7. The science teacher may want to teach an insect lesson following this library lesson.

## Learning Styles

Linguistic (recalling facts), spatial (coloring), and interpersonal (discussing)

## Teaching Team

Art, library, and science teachers

## Resources

Gibbons, Gail. *The Honey Makers*. New York: HarperCollins, 1997.

O'Toole, Christopher. *Discovering Bees and Wasps*. New York: Bookwright Press, 1986.

# The Elves and the Shoemaker

## Standards

Students will

- Demonstrate a knowledge of the plots and major characters of selected classic fairy tales, folktales, legends, and fables from around the world (McREL 6)

- Appreciate literature and other creative expressions (AASL/AECT 5)

## Objectives

After listening to *The Elves and the Shoemaker*, students evaluate its plot and characters. Students make a puzzle about the fairy tale.

## Directions

1. Copy the puzzle sheet onto heavier paper to make a more durable puzzle for students. The art teacher may want to teach the puzzle part of the lesson.

2. The library teacher reads *The Elves and the Shoemaker* fairy tale.

3. The class will discuss the plot and the characters.

4. Students make a puzzle featuring characters and activities in *The Elves and the Shoemaker*.

5. Students color their worksheet puzzles before cutting along the lines. (Remind students to be careful with the scissors.)

6. After cutting the puzzles apart, students practice putting their puzzles together.

7. Students may watch the video *The Shoemaker and the Elves* in language arts class as a re-inforcement of the fairy tale.

## Learning Styles

Spatial (puzzles and coloring) and intrapersonal (working alone)

## Teaching Team

Art, language arts, and library teachers

## Suggested Resources

Galdone, Paul. *The Elves and the Shoemaker*. New York: Clarion Books, 1984.

*The Shoemaker and the Elves*. Chicago: Films First, 1989 [video].

## Hare and Tortoise Television Show

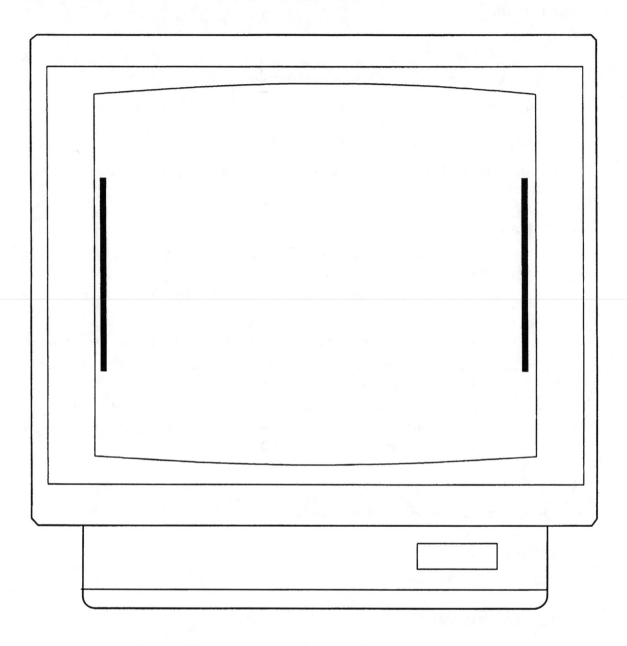

TV Producer _____

# The Hare and the Tortoise

1

## They raced.

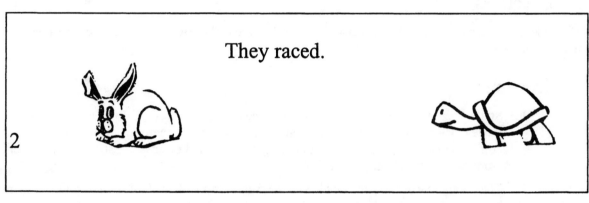

2

## The tortoise won.

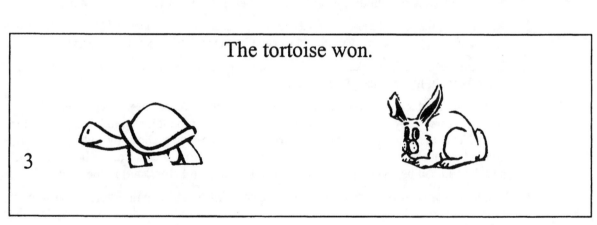

3

## Standards

Students will

- Demonstrate a knowledge of the plots and major characters of selected classic fairy tales, folktales, legends, and fables from around the world (McREL 6)

- Appreciate literature and other creative expressions (AASL/AECT 5)

- Strive for excellence information seeking (AASL/AECT 6)

- Practice ethical behavior in regard to information and technology (AASL/AECT 8)

## Objectives

Students discuss the plot, characters, and moral of the hare and the tortoise fable. Students color and create a fable television show.

## Directions

1. Students create a television show based on the hare and tortoise fable. (Cut out the slits on the television worksheet for the students ahead of time.) If there isn't time for students to create a television program, the students may color and discuss the strips on the second worksheet after listening to the fable.

2. The library teacher tells the fable of the hare and tortoise. This fable can be found in many books, including the children's fable of *The Aesop for Children* by Milo Winter.

3. After hearing the fable, the teacher and the students talk about what happened (the plot). They discuss the moral ("if you keep trying, you'll succeed") and the characters of the hare and the tortoise.

4. Students color their worksheets. They may make a television show fable from the worksheets in library class or in art class.

5. If students are creating a television show, remind them to be careful when using the art supplies. First, they cut out the three fable strips and tape them together into one long strip. Next, the students are ready to create their television show by pulling the strips gently through the precut, darkened lines of the television. If desired, the beginning strip and the end can be taped onto a straw cut in half once it is threaded in the television.

6. In language arts class, students may practice showing and telling their television show fable with peers. If students are not creating a television show, student pairs may tell each other the fable by showing the picture strips. They should practice telling the fable until they can tell the fable correctly.

## Learning Styles

Linguistic (telling a story), spatial (coloring), and bodily kinesthetic (crafts)

## Teaching Team

Art, language arts, and library teachers

## Suggested Resources

Ward, Helen. *Hare and Tortoise*. Brookfield, CT: Millbrook Press, 1999.

Winter, Milo. *The Aesop for Children*. New York: Barnes & Noble, 1993.

# Easter Hunt

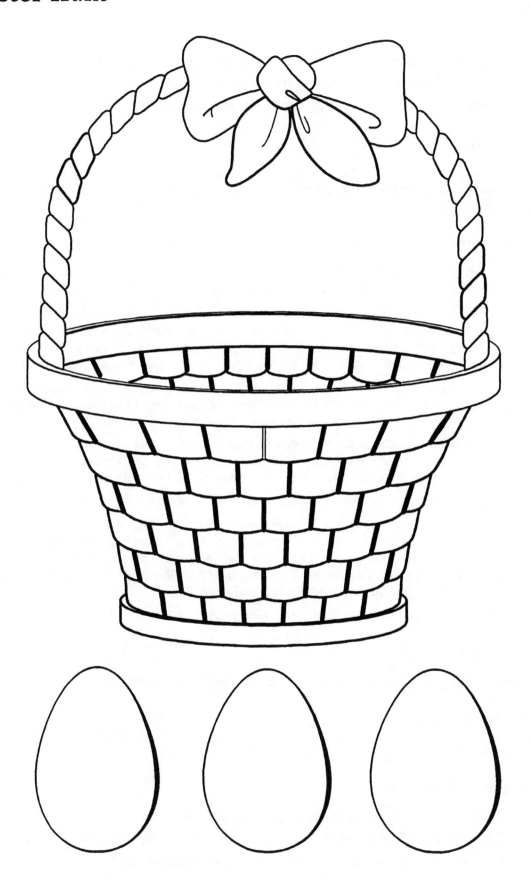

## Standards

Students will

- Demonstrate a basic familiarity with selected fiction and poetry (McREL 7)
- Access information efficiently and effectively (AASL/AECT 1)
- Pursue information related to personal interest (AASL/AECT 4)

## Objectives

Students listen to alphabet books. Students will recognize that fiction books are alphabetical. Students color and then glue worksheet baskets on sacks. Students will go on an egg hunt to collect alphabetical eggs from corresponding easy-reading shelves.

## Directions

1. This lesson should take place in the school library media center if possible because its purpose is to help students learn about fiction books and their location in the library.

2. Copy the eggs from the worksheet onto several sheets of colored construction paper so that each student will have five eggs. The teacher or an assistant writes an alphabet letter on each egg and then places the eggs on the corresponding easy-reading shelves. For instance, the "A" eggs should be hidden on the "A" shelves, the "B" eggs on the "B" shelves, and so on.

3. To introduce this lesson, the language arts teacher reads an ABC book, such as *The Alphabet Book* by P.D. Eastman in the classroom or at the start of library class. If possible, the library teacher reads *The Bunnies Alphabet Eggs* by Lisa Bassett.

4. The library teacher points out to students that easy-reading books are organized in alphabetical order. For example, the teacher points out that all of the Dr. Seuss books are on the "S" shelf. The teacher points out two or three other library shelf letters and their corresponding books.

5. Students color, cut out, and then glue the worksheet basket onto a small sack.

6. Students are ready for their Easter egg hunt. Students see if they can find the alphabet eggs from the easy-reading section. They place their eggs in their Easter baskets. Once the egg hunt is over, students chose an egg from their basket and then find a corresponding book from the easy-reading section. For example, if they choose a "B" egg from their basket, they look for a book on the "B" shelf, and so on.

7. Students may also play the *Curious George: ABC Adventure* CD-ROM.

## Learning Styles

Spatial (coloring), intrapersonal (working alone), and bodily kinesthetic (active)

## Teaching Team

Language arts and library teachers

## Suggested Resources

Bassett. Lisa. *The Bunnies Alphabet Eggs*. New York: Jelly Bean Press, 1993.

*Curious George: ABC Adventure*. Sommerville, MA: Houghton Mifflin Interactive, 1999 [CD-ROM].

Eastman, P.D. *The Alphabet Book*. New York: Random House, 2000.

# Old MacDonald Had a Farm

Help Old MacDonald get his animals back on his farm.

## Standards

Students will

- When prompted by the teacher, recite the texts of a variety of familiar rhymes (McREL 5)
- Appreciate literature and other creative expressions (AASL/AECT 5)
- Practice ethical behavior in regard to information and technology (AASL/AECT 8)

## Objectives

Students recite the familiar "Old MacDonald" rhyme. Students demonstrate the rhyme by coloring, cutting, and gluing farm animals onto MacDonald's farm.

## Directions

1. The music teacher may want to introduce the "Old MacDonald Had a Farm" rhyming song to students before library class.

2. The library teacher will locate the rhyme of "Old MacDonald Had a Farm" in book format (such as the book illustrated by Glen Rounds).

3. As the library teacher reads the rhyming book, students repeat the rhymes with the teacher. After listening to the book, students can make up their own rhymes with different animals.

4. Students help Old MacDonald find his farm animals on the farm worksheets. They will color and then cut out the animals and the barn.

5. Students glue the animals and the barn onto a blank sheet of paper in order to create a farm scene. They can also draw other animals on their farm.

6. When students are done with the worksheets, they can repeat the rhyme again.

7. As follow-up, students can listen to a different version of Old MacDonald written by Holly Berry. Students can also play the *Rights' Animal Farm* CD-ROM.

## Learning Styles

Linguistic (telling a story), musical, interpersonal (working alone), and spatial (art)

## Teaching Team

Library and music teachers

## Suggested Resources

Berry, Holly. *Old MacDonald Had a Farm*. New York: North-South Books, 1994.

*Rights' Animal Farm*. New York: Golden Books Powerhouse Entertainment, 1997 [CD-ROM].

Rounds, Glen. *Old MacDonald Had a Farm*. New York: Holiday House, 1989.

## Old Lady

The Old Lady—What did she swallow?

## Standards

Students will

- When prompted by teacher recite the texts of a variety of familiar rhymes (McREL 5)
- Demonstrate a basic familiarity with selected fiction and poetry (McREL 7)
- Appreciate literature and other creative expressions (AASL/AECT 5)

## Objectives

Students recognize characters after repeating the rhyme of "The Old Lady Who Swallowed a Fly." Students will be able to sequence plot order by gluing the characters onto the worksheet in order of their appearance in the story.

## Directions

1. The music teacher may have students sing the musical rendition of "There Was an Old Lady Who Swallowed a Fly" in music class as an introduction to the library lesson.
2. The library teacher reads the poem, "There Was an Old Lady Who Swallowed a Fly." (A popular version is the book by Simms Taback.)
3. After reading the poem, students look at the illustrations and discuss the characters.
4. The library teacher reads the poem again, as students recite it along with the teacher.
5. Students are given a worksheet with a picture of the old lady. They will color the various things that the old lady swallowed.
6. Students will cut out the things on their worksheet and then glue them onto the old lady.
7. Students look at their sheets and again recite the story with the library teacher.
8. This lesson could be followed-up by a sequencing lesson in math class.

## Learning Styles

Linguistic (telling the story), mathematical (sequencing), intrapersonal (working alone), and musical (the rhythm of the poem)

## Teaching Team

Library, math, and music teachers

## Suggested Resources

Taback, Simms. *There Was an Old Lady Who Swallowed a Fly*. New York: Viking, 1997.

## Pumpkins

## Standards

Students will

- Comprehend the basic plot of simple stories (McREL 3)
- Make simple inferences regarding "what will happen next" or "how things could have turned out differently" (McREL 4)
- Demonstrate a basic familiarity with selected fiction and poetry (McREL 7)
- Appreciate literature and other creative expressions (AASL/AECT 5)

## Objectives

Students predict what will happen in a fictional story about pumpkins. Students analyze the main plot and create a jack-o'-lantern.

## Directions

1. This lesson should be given around fall or Halloween, when classroom teachers have students visit pumpkin patches.
2. The library teacher gathers some easy-reading fiction books on pumpkins. (Some examples are *Big Pumpkin* by Erica Silverman, *Pumpkin Fair* by Eva Bunting, or *It's Pumpkin Time* by Zoe Hal.)
3. The library teacher reads and shows two pumpkin books to students. The teacher stops once in a while to ask students to guess what might happen next.
4. After hearing and listening to the books, the class will discuss the main plot or what happened in each book.
5. The class makes their own jack-o'-lanterns using the pumpkin worksheets. If time is limited, the class may simply color the pumpkins.
6. The art teacher may have students create papier-mâché jack-o'-lanterns in art class.

## Learning Styles

Linguistic (telling the story), spatial (designing and coloring), and intrapersonal (working alone)

## Teaching Team

Art, library, and main classroom teachers

## Suggested Resources

Bunting, Eve. *Pumpkin Fair*. New York: Clarion Books, 1997.

Hall, Zoe. *It's Pumpkin Time*. New York: Clarion Books, 1997.

Silverman, Erica. *Big Pumpkin*. New York: Simon & Schuster, 1992.

## The Gingerbread Boy

Run, run, as fast as you can.
You can't catch me,
I'm the Gingerbread Boy.

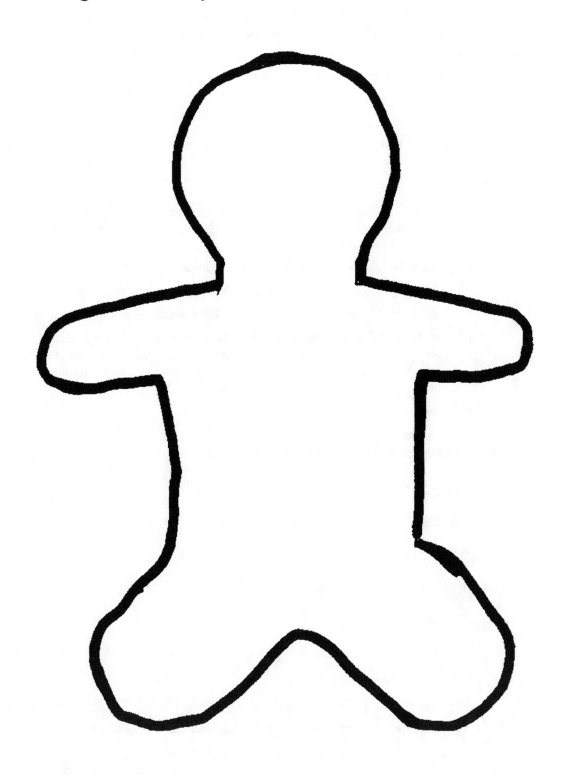

## Standards

Students will

- Make simple inferences regarding "what will happen next" or "how things could have turned out differently" (McREL 4)
- When prompted by the teacher, recite the texts of a variety of familiar rhymes (McREL 5)
- Demonstrate a knowledge of the plots and major characters of selected fairy tales, folktales, legends, and fables from around the world (McREL 6)
- Appreciate literature and other creative expressions (AASL/AECT 5)
- Participate effectively in groups to pursue and generate information (AASL/AECT 9)

## Objectives

Students recite rhymes. Students deduce and then illustrate inferences for a different story ending.

## Directions

1. The library teacher reads one of the familiar Gingerbread Boy or Gingerbread Man books. (One example is the *Gingerbread Boy* retold by David Cutts. Another example is found in *Childcraft Encyclopedia*.)

2. Students recite some of the character refrains as the teacher reads.

3. After hearing the book, students discuss plot and main characters.

4. Then students discuss how things might have turned out differently in the end.

5. On the worksheets, students will drawing directly on the Gingerbread Boy, illustrating how things might have turned out differently. For example, students may say that the Gingerbread Boy decided to trick the fox. If they choose this ending, students draw a picture of the fox being outsmarted on the Gingerbread Boy.

6. Students share their new endings with the class.

7. In language arts class, students may watch the *Gingerbread Man* in video format after reviewing plot and characters from the story.

## Learning Styles

Linguistic (telling the story), interpersonal (sharing), and spatial (illustrating)

## Teaching Team

Language arts and library teachers

## Suggested Resources

*Childcraft Encyclopedia: The How and Why Library*. Chicago: World Book, 2000.

Cook, Scott. *Gingerbread Boy*. New York: Dragonfly Books, 1996.

Cutts, David. *Gingerbread Boy*. Mahwah, NJ: Troll, 1989.

*Gingerbread Man*. Pine Plains, NY: Live Oaks Media, 1994 [video].

Kimmel, Eric. *The Gingerbread Man*. New York: Holiday House, 1993.

# My Animal Rhymes

*My Animal Rhymes*

by:

Mary had a little lamb,
Its fleece was white as snow
And everywhere that Mary went
The lamb was sure to go.

Hey diddle diddle,
The cat and the fiddle,
The cow jumped over the moon.
The little dog laughed
To see such sport, and
The dish ran away with the spoon.

Hickory, dickory, dock,
The mouse ran up the clock.
The clock struck one,
The mouse ran down,
Hickory, dickory, dock.

## Standards

Students will

- Use pictures clues and picture captions as an aid to comprehension (McREL 2)
- When prompted by the teacher, recite the texts of a variety of familiar rhymes (McREL 5)
- Demonstrate a basic familiarity with selected fiction and poetry (McREL 7)
- Appreciate literature and other creative expressions (AASL/AECT 5)

## Objectives

Students recall familiar Mother Goose rhymes. Students color and construct simple nursery rhyme booklets.

## Directions

1. The library teacher collects Mother Goose nursery rhymes. (Some books featuring Mother Goose rhymes include *Marguerite de Angeli's Book of Nursery and Mother Goose Rhymes* and Lucy Cousins's Mother Goose book called *The Little Dog Laughed*.)
2. The teacher reads some simple rhymes and has the class repeat the rhymes from nursery rhyme books and then from student worksheets.
3. Students color and cut out the two rhyme worksheets.
4. The worksheets will be stapled together to make a rhyming animal booklet.
5. Once the books are completed, the class repeats the rhymes from their new booklets as they look at the illustrations for picture clues.
6. The music teacher may have the students bring their booklets to music class so the students can sing their rhymes while looking at their booklets.
7. This lesson creates a nice follow-up for Mother Goose nursery rhymes taught in language arts.

## Learning Styles

Linguistic (read and tell rhymes), intrapersonal (working alone), spatial (coloring), and musical (rhythm)

## Teaching Team

Language arts, library, and music teachers

## Suggested Resources

Any collection of Mother Goose nursery rhymes.

Cousins, Lucy. *The Little Dog Laughed*. New York: Penguin, 1995.

de Angeli, Marguerite. *Marguerite de Angeli's Book of Nursery and Mother Goose Rhymes*. New York: Doubleday, 1954.

Wildsmith, Brian (illustrator). *Mother Goose*. Oxford, England: Oxford University Press, 1987.

## Shapes of Things

## Standards

Students will

- Use picture clues and picture captions as an aid to comprehension (McREL 2)
- Access information efficiently and effectively (AASL/AECT 1)
- Use information accurately and creatively (AASL/AECT 3)
- Pursue information related to personal interest (AASL/AECT 4)

## Objectives

Students analyze mathematical shapes while listening to and looking at shape books. Students design objects from colored shapes.

## Directions

1. The library teacher will read one or two books on shapes. Some examples of shape books are *Color Zoo* by Lois Ehlert, *Shapes, Shapes, Shapes* by Tana Hoban, and *Shapes* by Sally Hewitt.
2. Students study the shapes shown in the book(s).
3. Then students design their own animal or object by using the shapes from the worksheet.
4. After deciding what to create, students draw a simple outline of their shape on a blank sheet of paper. Then students color, cut out, and glue their shapes on their outline.
5. The library teacher can label the animal or object on each student paper.
6. Student designs can be displayed on the bulletin board.
7. As a reinforcement, the math teacher may have students play the shapes part of the *Math Blaster* CD-ROM for grades Pre-K–1 in math class.

## Learning Styles

Mathematical (thinking logically), intrapersonal (working alone), and spatial (designing)

## Teaching Team

Math and library teachers

## Suggested Resources

Ehlert, Lois. *Color Zoo*. New York: J. B. Lippincott, 1989.

Hewitt, Sally. *Shapes*. Austin, TX: Steck-Vaughn, 1996.

Hoban, Tana. *Shapes, Shapes, Shapes*. New York: Greenwillow Books, 1986.

*Math Blaster*. New Jersey: Knowledge Adventures, 2000 [CD-ROM].

# Squirrels

## Standards

Students will

- Use picture clues and picture captions as an aide to comprehension (McREL 2)
- Demonstrate a basic familiarity with selected fiction and poetry (McREL 7)
- Demonstrate a basic familiarity with selected works of nonfiction (McREL 8)
- Access information efficiently and effectively (AASL/AECT 1)
- Evaluate information critically and competently (AASL/AECT 2)
- Use information accurately and creatively (AASL/AECT 3)
- Pursue information related to personal interest (AASL/AECT 4)

## Objectives

Students gather facts about squirrels while listening to facts from an encyclopedia. Students illustrate and color squirrel dwellings.

## Directions

1. To introduce the lesson on squirrels, the library teacher reads one or two fiction books about squirrels. (Two easy-reading books are *Nuts to You!* by Lois Ehlert or *Night Gliders* by Joanna Ryder.)

2. The teacher asks students if they have some questions about squirrels that can be discovered with today's research. Then the teacher will look up the answers to student's questions in an encyclopedia. (The teacher also may simply tell the students two or three facts about squirrels from the encyclopedia.) Facts might include what squirrels eat and where they dwell.

3. The teacher shows the students illustrations of squirrel dwellings.

4. On their squirrel worksheets, students illustrate dwellings. Students will draw a tree or something similar for squirrels to sit upon, according to the encyclopedia facts.

5. Students color their squirrel worksheets.

6. If students have access to a computer lab, students can draw their trees and squirrels with the *Kid Pix* computer program instead of using the worksheets.

7. In science class, the teacher may have students learn more about squirrels by looking at the pictures from either an encyclopedia or a nonfiction easy reader, such as the *Flying Squirrels* book by Lynn Stone.

## Learning Styles

Spatial (drawing, coloring) and interpersonal (group work)

## Teaching Team

Library and science teachers

## Suggested Resources

Ehlert, Lois. *Nuts to You!* San Diego, CA: Harcourt Brace Jovanovich, 1993.

*Kid Pix* [computer drawing program]. Novato, CA: Learning Company, 2001.

Ryder, Joanna. *Night Gliders*. Mahwah, NJ: Troll, 1996.

Stone, Lynn M. *Flying Squirrels*. Vero Beach, FL: Rourke, 1993.

*World Book Encyclopedia*. Chicago: World Book, 2001.

**Thanksgiving**

I am thankful for:

## Standards

Students will

- Demonstrate a basic familiarity with selected fiction and poetry (McREL 7)
- Demonstrate a basic familiarity with selected works of nonfiction (McREL 8)
- Access information efficiently and effectively (AASL/AECT 1)
- Evaluate information critically and competently (AASL/AECT 2)
- Recognize the importance of information to a democratic society (AASL/AECT 7)
- Participate effectively in groups to pursue and generate information (AASL/AECT 9)

## Objectives

Students search and then discuss things for which they are thankful. Students create Thanksgiving cards.

## Directions

1. If students are going to make a Thanksgiving card, the art or library teacher should copy both Thanksgiving worksheets on card stock or heavy paper. If students are not going to make a card, they can simply use the turkeys as worksheets. The art teacher can direct the Thanksgiving card activity.

2. The library teacher locates some nonfiction books about Thanksgiving (such as *1, 2, 3 Thanksgiving!* by W. Nikola-Lisa or *Thanksgiving Day* by Gail Gibbons). The teacher locates a Thanksgiving fiction book (such as *My First Thanksgiving* by Tomie dePaola).

3. The library teacher reads the Thanksgiving books to the class while pointing out things for which people are thankful.

4. The class will discuss different things for which they are thankful.

5. Students draw what they are thankful for on their Thanksgiving cards or worksheets.

6. Students color the card sheet or worksheet that says "Happy Thanksgiving."

7. If making a card, the art or library teacher tapes or staples the two card parts together.

8. This lesson will harmonize with the social studies teacher's Thanksgiving lesson to create a nice conclusion for that lesson.

## Learning Styles

Spatial (drawing and coloring), interpersonal (working together), and intrapersonal (working alone)

## Teaching Team

Art, library, and social studies teachers

## Suggested Resources

dePaola, Tomie. *My First Thanksgiving*. New York: Putnam, 1992.

Gibbons, Gail. *Thanksgiving Day*. New York: Holiday House, 1983.

Nikola-Lisa, W. *1, 2, 3 Thanksgiving!* Morton Grove, IL: Whitman, 1991.

# 'Twas the Night Before Christmas

'Twas the night before Christmas,
And all through the house,
Not a creature was stirring, but just a wee mouse!

## Standards

Students will

- Use picture clues and picture captions as an aide to comprehension (McREL 2)
- Make simple inferences regarding "what will happen next" or "how things could have turned out differently" (McREL 4)
- Demonstrate a basic familiarity with selected fiction and poetry (McREL 7)
- Appreciate literature and other creative expressions (AASL/AECT 5)

## Objectives

Students use picture clues to understand plot and characters of a traditional Christmas story poem. Students reconstruct a different story ending and then color the main characters involved in their new ending.

## Directions

1. In this lesson, *The Night Before Christmas* is told from a different point of view—that of the mouse.

2. First, the library teacher reads the story poem, *The Night Before Christmas* from an illustrated children's book. (One example is the book illustrated by Elizabeth Miles.) While reading the story poem, the teacher will stop to show all the illustrations to help students understand the poem.

3. The class will discuss what might happen if the Santa character saw a mouse waiting for him.

4. Students color the Christmas worksheet. If this sheet is laminated after students have colored it, it could be made into a Christmas place mat. The art teacher may have another idea for a place mat of Santa and his mouse to be completed in art class.

5. In language arts class, students can listen to a Christmas mouse story (such as *The Mouse Before Christmas* by Michael Garland or *The Tiny Christmas Elf* by Sharon Peters).

## Learning Styles

Linguistic (discussing the story), spatial (coloring and creating), and musical (poetry rhythm)

## Teaching Team

Art, language arts, and library teachers

## Suggested Resources

Garland, Michael. *The Mouse Before Christmas*. New York: E. P. Dutton, 1997.

Moore, Clement, and Elizabeth Miles (illustrator). *'Twas the Night Before Christmas*. New York: HarperCollins, 1999.

Peters, Sharon. *The Tiny Christmas Elf*. Mahwah, NJ: Troll, 1988.

# Tigers

# Standards

Students will

- Understand that reading is a way of gaining information about the world (McREL 1)
- Demonstrate a basic familiarity with selected works of nonfiction (McREL 8)
- Access information efficiently and effectively (AASL/AECT 1)
- Evaluate information critically and competently (AASL/AECT 2)
- Use information accurately and creatively (AASL/AECT 3)
- Practice ethical behavior in regard to information and information technology (AASL/AECT 8)

# Objectives

Students discover facts about tigers while listening to facts from a nonfiction source. Students create tiger masks.

# Directions

1. The library teacher copies the Tigers worksheets onto white construction paper or card stock so the students can make masks out of the worksheets.

2. The library or science teacher reads brief facts about tigers from a nonfiction easy-reading source (such as *Tigers* by Lynn Stone). The teacher can also use an encyclopedia if a nonfiction book is unavailable.

3. As the teacher reads brief tiger facts, he or she should point out the tiger's colors. The teacher lists the colors (black and orange) on the board (kindergarten students should be able to read color words).

4. Students will color the tigers according to the color words listed on the board, tracing the tiger's stripes with the black color.

5. Student masks can be attached with ribbon or yarn. However, students can simply hold their masks in front of their faces.

6. In language arts class, students can act out a tiger fiction story using their masks. The English teacher may wish to read books about tigers aloud (such as *Tigers* by Roland Edwards or *Tiger Is a Scaredy Cat* by Joan Phillips). Students should be reminded to be "quiet tigers" in the classroom.

# Learning Styles

Spatial (imagining, coloring), intrapersonal (working alone), and bodily kinesthetic (acting)

# Teaching Team

Language arts, library, and science teachers

# Suggested Resources

Edwards, Roland. *Tigers*. New York: Tambourine Books, 1992.

Phillips, Joan. *Tiger Is a Scaredy Cat*. New York: Random House, 1986.

Stone, Lynn. *Tigers*. Vero Beach, FL: Rourke, 1989.

**Be My Valentine**

# Standards

Students will

- Comprehend the basic plot of simple stories (McREL 3)
- Demonstrate a basic familiarity with selected fiction and poetry (McREL 7)
- Appreciate literature and other creative expressions (AASL/AECT 5)
- Participate effectively in groups to pursue and generate information (AASL/AECT 9)

# Objectives

Students discuss characters from fiction books by the same author and that feature dogs as the main characters. Students compare plots of the books. Students color Valentine bookmarks.

# Directions

1. The library teacher copies the Valentine worksheets on light pink or heavy white paper to make bookmarks.
2. The teacher chooses books by the same author for the day's author study. The teacher reads either Norman Bridwell's Clifford books or Cynthia Rylant's Henry and Mudge books.
3. The teacher reads two books by the selected author, such as *Clifford's Puppy Days*, *Clifford's First Valentine Day*, *Clifford's Pals*, *Clifford's Family*, and *Clifford the Small Red Puppy*. Henry and Mudge books include *Henry and Mudge*, *Henry and Mudge and the Happy Cat*, *Henry and Mudge and the Sneaky Crackers*, and *Henry and Mudge and the Wild Wind*.
4. After listening to the two books, the class discusses the plots and the dog characters.
5. Students color their Valentine bookmarks. Depending on which books the students heard, they should color their dog to look like Clifford or like Mudge.
6. Tell students that they will give their bookmarks to someone special as a Valentine.
7. To reinforce literary skills, the language arts teacher can read another Clifford or Henry and Mudge book and discuss plot and character.

# Learning Styles

Spatial (coloring), intrapersonal (working alone), interpersonal (working together), and linguistic (discussing)

# Teaching Team

Language arts and library teachers

# Suggested Resources

Bridwell, Norman. *Clifford's Family*. New York: Scholastic, 1984.

Bridwell, Norman. *Clifford's First Valentine Day*. New York: Scholastic, 1997.

Bridwell, Norman. *Clifford's Pals*. New York: Scholastic, 1985.

Bridwell, Norman. *Clifford's Puppy Days*. New York: Scholastic, 1989.

Rylant, Cynthia. *Henry and Mudge and the Happy Cat*. New York: Simon & Schuster, 1990.

Rylant, Cynthia. *Henry and Mudge and the Sneaky Crackers*. New York: Simon & Schuster, 1998.

Rylant, Cynthia. *Henry and Mudge and the Wild Wind*. New York: Aladdin, 1996.

# Three Bears

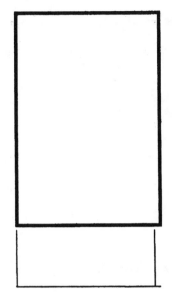

## Standards

Students will

- Demonstrate a knowledge of the plots and major characters of selected classic fairy tales, folktales, legends, and fables from around the world (McREL 6)
- Appreciate literature and other creative expressions (AASL/AECT 5)

## Objectives

Students identify plot and characters from *Goldilocks and the Three Bears*. Students color and create characters to act out the fairy tale.

## Directions

1. This library lesson may follow a language arts unit on fairy tales.
2. The library teacher reads *Goldilocks and the Three Bears* aloud to the students. (This tale can be found in the *Childcraft Encyclopedia* or in other easy-reading books, such as *Goldilocks and the Three Bears* illustrated by James Marshall.)
3. If students are familiar with the story, they can recite each bear's refrain with the teacher.
4. After hearing the book, the class will discuss the plots and characters.
5. On the bear worksheets, students design their own Goldilocks (or another character) to act out the story.
6. Students cut out the characters, bending them on the dotted lines so that the cutouts can be placed in a standing position.
7. In small groups, students act out the story using their character cutouts.
8. The art teacher may have students design a shoe-box stage for student's characters during the next art class.

## Learning Styles

Linguistic (telling the story), spatial (coloring and drawing), and bodily kinesthetic (acting)

## Teaching Team

Art, language arts, and library teachers

## Suggested Resources

*Childcraft Encyclopedia: The How and Why Library*. Chicago: World Book, 2000.

Marshall, James. *Goldilocks and the Three Bears*. New York: Dial Books for Young Readers, 1998.

# Chapter 2

## First-Grade Lesson Plans

In order to create solid professional-based library lesson plans, the following selected Kendall and Marzano or McREL National Education Standards and Benchmarks for Kindergarten were chosen from the area of language arts, as it directly correlates with library information and appreciation skills. Furthermore, the AASL (American Association of School Libraries) and the AECT (Association for Educational Communications and Technology) list of Information Literacy Standards were applied to every lesson to ensure that all students will develop literary appreciation and will be effective users of information and ideas (listed in the Introduction). Teaching objectives were also given for each lesson as linked to the standards or active goals. Finally, Gardner's multiple intelligences are also integrated into each lesson, as all students have different methods of learning (also listed in the Introduction).

*Each lesson plan has a direct reference to the following numbered McREL benchmarks under the corresponding standards, as well as a direct reference to AASL/AECT standards. Finally, all of the following twenty-minute lesson plans should be used in conjunction with the other teachers whenever possible. Moreover, all lesson plans are not the only means, but some of many, for library instruction. The following lessons can provide whole group discussion ideas, or they can provide individual or small group worksheet work.*

# First-Grade Library Standards and Language Arts Benchmarks (McREL)*

First-grade students will be able to

- Demonstrate competence in the general skills and strategies of the reading process (Standard 5)

    1.   Understand reading is a way of gaining information about the world

    2.   Use picture clues and picture captions as an aid to comprehension

- Demonstrate competence in general skills and strategies for reading literature (Standard 6)

    3.   Comprehend the basic plot of simple stories

    4.   Make simple inference regarding "what will happen next" or "how things could have turned out differently"

    5.   Become aware of the geographic information important to the stories one reads (for grades 3–5)

    6.   Share responses to literature with peers (for grades 3–5)

    7.   Identify the main characters in works containing only a few basic characters (for grades 3–5)

- Demonstrate a familiarity with selected literary works of enduring quality (Standard 13)

    8.   When prompted by the teacher, recite the texts of a variety of familiar rhymes

    9.   Demonstrate knowledge of the plots and major characters of selected classic fairy tales, folktales, legends, and fables from around the world

    10.   Demonstrate a basic familiarity with selected fiction and poetry

    11.   Demonstrate a basic familiarity with selected works of nonfiction

**Very Good Berry Rhymes**

----------------------------------------------------------------

----------------------------------------------------------------

----------------------------------------------------------------

----------------------------------------------------------------

## Standards

Students will

- Demonstrate a basic familiarity with selected fiction and poetry (McREL 10)
- Appreciate literature and other creative expressions (AASL/AECT 5)

## Objectives

Students become familiar with rhymes. Students learn and write a brief rhyme on their berry worksheets.

## Directions

1. The library teacher gathers rhymes about berries. (*Jamberry* by Bruce Degen includes simple and fun berry rhymes.) The language arts teacher may wish to co-teach.

2. The library teacher will discuss the illustrations associated with each rhyme before reading each one.

3. The library teacher writes one or two of the very short rhyme(s) on the board. The class repeats the rhyme(s).

4. Students write a rhyme on their berry sheets. They may copy a rhyme from the board, or they may create their own rhyme patterned after those in the book.

5. Students color their worksheets.

6. The class repeats some of the learned rhymes.

7. The music teacher may want to follow-up this lesson plan by having students listen to and then repeat the rhymes from the *Jamberry* audio tape.

## Learning Styles

Linguistic (reading and writing), spatial (coloring), interpersonal (working together), and musical (rhythm of rhymes)

## Teaching Team

Language arts, library, and music teachers

## Suggested Resources

Degen, Bruce. *Jamberry*. New York: Harper & Row, 1983.

*Jamberry*. New York: Scholastic, 1995 [audio tape].

**Bremen Town Musicians**

 **Dog**

 **Donkey**

 **Rooster**

 **Cat**

## Standards

Students will

- Share responses to literature with peers (McREL 6)
- Demonstrate a knowledge of the plots and major characteristics of selected classic fairy tales, folktales, legends, and fables from around the world (McREL 9)
- Appreciate literature and other creative expressions (AASL/AECT 5)
- Participate effectively in groups to pursue and generate information (AASL/AECT 9)

## Objectives

Students identify and color the characters from the Bremen Town Musicians after hearing the story. Students will act out the plots of the story.

## Directions

1. Copy the Bremen Town Musicians character worksheets on heavy paper.
2. The library teacher reads a version of the Bremen Town Musicians folktale.
3. The class identifies the main characters and the plot of the folktale.
4. Give students a few minutes to color and cut out the character strips.
5. Select four students to act out the folktale's plot while holding the character strips.
6. The students act out the story while the library teacher repeats the main plot. (For example, the students could act out the animals meeting each other, looking in the robbers' house, scaring the robbers, and then living happily ever after.)
7. Students may enjoy viewing the *Bremen Town Musicians* video in language arts class as follow-up to this lesson.

## Learning Styles

Bodily kinesthetic (acting), interpersonal (working together), and spatial (coloring)

## Teaching Team

Language arts and library teachers

## Suggested Resources

*Bremen Town Musicians*. Phoenix, AZ: BFA, 1981 [video].

Gross, Ruth Belov. *Bremen Town Musicians*. New York: Scholastic, 1981.

Plume, Ilse. *Bremen Town Musicians*. New York: Bantam Doubleday, 1980.

# The Lion and the Mouse

The mouse said, "Do not eat me."

"Help," roared the lion.

"Thank you for helping me," said the lion.

Covers

The Lion and the Mouse

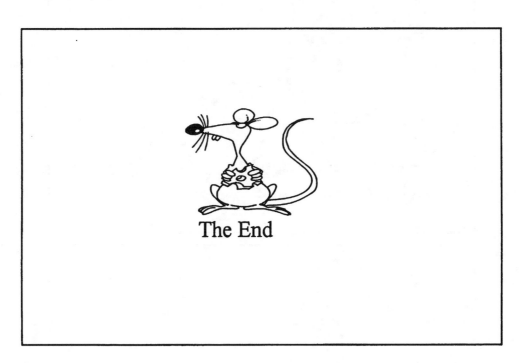

The End

# Standards

Students will

- Use picture clues and picture captions as an aid to comprehension (McREL 2)
- Demonstrate a knowledge of the plots and major characters of selected classic fairy tales, folktales, legends, and fables from around the world (McREL 9)
- Appreciate literature and other creative expressions (AASL/AECT 5)
- Strive for excellence in information seeking (AASL/AECT 6)
- Practice ethical behavior in regard to information and information technology (AASL/AECT 8)

# Objectives

Students locate plot and characters of the lion and the mouse fable after hearing it. Students produce booklets of the fable.

# Directions

1. The library teacher reads "The Lion and the Mouse" fable. As the book is being read, students should be given the opportunity to examine the pictures.
2. After hearing the story, the class will discuss the plot and the two main characters. The teacher explains the moral of the story ("you never know who can help you").
3. Students make their own lion and mouse fable booklets from the worksheet pages included here. (The booklet covers are included on one of the worksheet pages, and the story is found on the other.) The art teacher may teach this part of the lesson.
4. The teacher reminds students to be careful using art tools. Students cut out their booklets and staple them together.
5. Students color their lion and mouse booklets.
6. During language arts class, student pairs may read their booklets to each other until they have learned the story. The lesson may precede or follow the language arts teacher's lessons on fables.

# Learning Styles

Linguistic (telling a story), spatial (coloring), and interpersonal (working in groups)

# Teaching Team

Art, language art, and library teachers

# Suggested Resources

Dole, Bob, Illustrator. *The Lion and the Mouse*. Mahwah, NJ: Troll, 1989.

Herman, Gail. *Lion and the Mouse*. New York: Random House, 1998.

Jones, Carol. *Lion and the Mouse*. Boston: Houghton Mifflin, 1997.

# The Little Red Hen

What is the story of the Little Red Hen?

## Standards

Students will

- Demonstrate a knowledge of the plots and major characters of selected classic fairy tales, folktales, legends, and fables from around the world (McREL 9)

- Make simple inferences regarding "what will happen next" or "how things could have turned out differently" (McREL 4)

- Appreciate literature and other creative expressions (AASL/AECT 5)

## Objectives

Students predict different story parts of *The Little Red Hen* folktale while listening to it. Students will illustrate the main plot on the worksheet bread.

## Directions

1. The library teacher reads *The Little Red Hen*.
2. As this book is being read, the teacher should pause to ask the class, "What will happen next?" The teacher shows students the pictures to verify the "next happenings" in the book.
3. After hearing the story, the teacher initiates a class discussion about the character of *The Little Red Hen*.
4. The class will discuss what the story was all about (the plot).
5. Students illustrate the plot on the slice of bread from the hen worksheet.
6. The language arts teacher may wish to follow up with a different version during a folktale lesson. The teacher could read and discuss *The Little Red Hen Makes a Pizza*.

## Learning Styles

Linguistic (listening to stories), intrapersonal (working alone), and spatial (drawing)

## Teaching Team

Language arts and library teachers

## Suggested Resources

Any version of *The Little Red Hen*.

Galdone, Paul. *The Little Red Hen*. New York: Houghton Mifflin, 1979.

Philemon, Sturges. *The Little Red Hen Makes a Pizza*. New York: Dutton Children's Books, 1999.

Ziefert, Harriet. *The Little Red Hen*. New York: Viking, 1995.

# A Paris Postcard

To:

Madeline

Paris, France

Read about Madeline. Then write to her.

# Standards

Students will

- Understand that reading is a way of gaining information about the world (McREL 1)
- Use pictures clues and picture captions as an aid to comprehension (McREL 2)
- Become aware of the geographic information important to the stories one reads (McREL 5)
- Appreciate literature and other creative expressions (AASL/AECT 5)
- Pursue information related to personal interest (AASL/AECT 4)
- Recognize the importance of information to a democratic society (AASL/AECT 7)

# Objectives

Students identify the geographic location and plot of a Madeline story after hearing it. Students identify the character, Madeline, and her antics and then write and illustrate a postcard to her.

# Directions

1.  Before the library lesson, the social studies teacher points out the location of Paris, France, on a map or in an atlas. The teacher shows illustrations of France from the Madeline books and other French resources.
2.  If desired, the teacher copies the postcards onto stiff paper.
3.  The library teacher reads one of Bemelman's Madeline books, such as *Madeline's Rescue, Madeline and the Bad Hat, Madeline and the Gypsies,* or *Madeline.*
4.  A French teacher may visit and teach students two or more French words.
5.  The class explains Madeline's antics. Students "write" a one-line postcard to Madeline to comment on her antics in Paris.
6.  On the front of the postcards, students can draw and color a picture of Paris as seen from one of the Madeline books or from a book about France.
7.  As a follow-up, students may watch *Madeline: The Musical* video in music class.
8.  Students may also play the *Madeline Thinking Games Deluxe* computer math game in math class.

# Learning Styles

Linguistic (writing), intrapersonal (working alone), musical (rhythm), and spatial (coloring)

# Teaching Team

French, library, math, music, and social studies teachers

# Suggested Resources

Bemelman, Ludvig. *Madeline*. New York: Viking, 1967.

Bemelman, Ludvig. *Madeline and the Bad Hat*. New York: Viking, 1984.

Bemelman, Ludvig. *Madeline and the Gypsies*. New York: Puffin Books, 1958.

Bemelman, Ludvig. *Madeline in London*. New York: Puffin Books, 1961.

Bemelman, Ludvig. *Madeline's Rescue*. New York: Viking, 1953.

*Madeline: The Musical*. New York: Ambrose, 1989 [video].

*Madeline's Thinking Games Deluxe*. Knoxville, TN: Creative Wonders, 1998 [CD-ROM].

## Paul Bunyan and His Ox

1. What would the ox say about Paul Bunyan:

_____

_____

2. Color the ox blue.

## Standards

Students will

- Identify the main characters in works containing only a few basic characters (McREL 7)

- Demonstrate a knowledge of the plots and major characters of selected classic fairy tales, folktales, legends, and fables from around the world (McREL 9)

- Appreciate information and other creative expressions (AASL/AECT 5)

## Objectives

Students understand what makes up a legend. Students discuss characters and plots from the legend of Paul Bunyan. Students describe Paul Bunyan on worksheets.

## Directions

1. The library teacher reads the legend of Paul Bunyan and Babe the Blue Ox. The teacher shows pictures from an easy-reading Paul Bunyan book while reading it out loud. (An example of an easy-reading Paul Bunyan book is Paul Orlando's *Paul Bunyan and Babe the Blue Ox.*)

2. After listening to the legend, the class discusses the plot.

3. After hearing the legend, the class will discuss the characters.

4. The teacher asks the class to think of short phrases to describe Paul Bunyan. The teacher writes these on the board. (For example, Paul was strong. Paul ate a lot. Paul worked hard. Paul was very big!)

5. Students copy these descriptive phrases onto their ox worksheet.

6. Students color the ox blue.

7. This library lesson could introduce legends for the language arts teacher in the main classroom, where students could watch the video *Paul Bunyan.*

## Learning Styles

Linguistic (writing) and spatial (coloring)

## Teaching Team

Language arts and library teachers

## Suggested Resources

Any resources that include the Paul Bunyan story.

Kellogg, Steven. *Paul Bunyan and the Blue Ox.* New York: William Morrow, 1984.

Orlando, Paul. *Paul Bunyan and Babe the Blue Ox.* St. Petersburg, FL: Worthington Press, 1995.

*Paul Bunyan.* Lincoln, NE: Reading Rainbow, 1984 [video].

# Thanksgiving

Color and cut out the pictures. Glue them in order of how Thanksgiving took place, as shown in the nonfiction books.

1.

2.

3.

4.

## Standards

Students will

- Demonstrate a basic familiarity with selected works of nonfiction (McREL 11)
- Access information efficiently and effectively (AASL/AECT 1)
- Evaluate information critically and competently (AASL/AECT 2)
- Use information accurately and creatively (AASL/AECT 3)
- Strive for excellence in information seeking (AASL/AECT 6)

## Objectives

Students review the history of Thanksgiving Day from nonfiction books. Students discuss the historical sequences that led to Thanksgiving Day. Students glue the historical sequence of events onto the Thanksgiving Day worksheets.

## Directions

1. After the social studies teacher has covered the history of Thanksgiving Day, the library teacher reinforces the history concept in library class.

2. The library teacher collects some easy-reading nonfiction sources about Thanksgiving. (One example is Gail Gibbons's book *Thanksgiving Day*.)

3. The teacher reads to students about the origin of Thanksgiving from nonfiction books.

4. The teacher explains the events that led to Thanksgiving.

5. The teacher gives small groups the opportunity to look at the illustrations in the Thanksgiving sources. The teacher points out the historical perspectives of Native Americans' lifestyles during this era in history.

6. The class reviews the events that led to Thanksgiving.

7. Students color the Thanksgiving worksheets and then glue the events in order of how they happened using the historical sequences described in the nonfiction sources. The teacher will ask students to verify their worksheets for understanding.

8. The math teacher may follow this library lesson with a math lesson on sequencing.

## Learning Styles

Linguistic (recalling facts), intrapersonal (working alone), and spatial (coloring)

## Teaching Team

Library, math, and social studies teachers

## Suggested Resources

Dalgiesh, Alice. *Thanksgiving Story*. New York: Charles Scribner's Sons, 1988.

Gibbons, Gail. *Thanksgiving Day*. New York: Holiday House, 1983.

Landau, Elaine. *Thanksgiving Day: A Time to Be Thankful*. Berkeley Heights, NJ: Enslow, 2001.

## Christmas Tree

Can you decorate this tree?

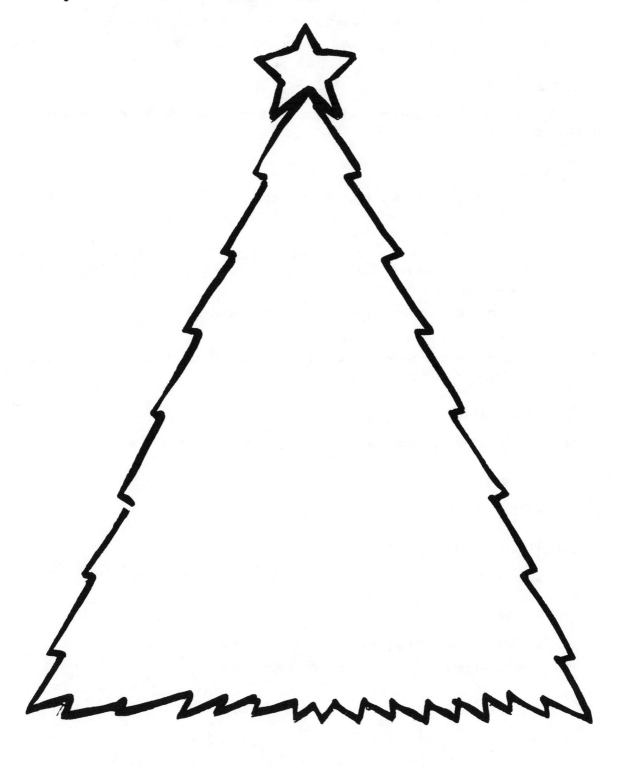

## Standards

Students will

- Comprehend the basic plot of simple stories (McREL 3)
- Demonstrate a familiarity with selected fiction and poetry (McREL 10)
- Appreciate literature and other creative expressions (AASL/AECT 5)

## Objectives

Students compare plots from different Christmas tree fiction stories. Students decorate Christmas tree ornaments.

## Directions

1. The art teacher may teach the ornament portion of this activity. The teacher may copy the Christmas trees onto stiff paper if the students are making tree ornaments. Otherwise the sheets can be copied onto regular paper.
2. The library teacher reads two or three easy-reading books about Christmas trees. (Some examples are *The Tree That Came to Stay, The Year of the Perfect Tree,* and *The Little Christmas Star.*)
3. After hearing the books, students will discuss the plots.
4. Students decorate the worksheet trees.
5. Students may simply wish to design their own Christmas trees with the *Kid Pix* computer program in art class.

## Learning Styles

Linguistic (discussing), intrapersonal (working alone), and spatial (art)

## Teaching Team

Art and library teachers

## Suggested Resources

Craig, Janet. *Little Christmas Star.* Mahwah, NJ: Troll, 1988.

Houston, Gloria. *The Year of the Perfect Tree.* New York: Dial Books for Young Readers, 1988.

*Kid Pix* [computer drawing program]. Novato, CA: Learning Company, 2001.

Quindlen, Anna. *The Tree That Came to Stay.* New York: Crown, 1992.

## Three Billy Goats

## Standards

Students will

- Demonstrate a knowledge of the plots and major characters of selected fairy tales, folktales, legends, and fables from around the world (McREL 9)

- Appreciate literature and other creative expressions (AASL/AECT 5)

## Objectives

Students listen to *The Three Billy Goats Gruff*. Students explain the plot and characters from the fairy tale. Students create Billy Goats Gruff puppets and then put on a puppet show.

## Directions

1. After the language arts teacher has covered fairy tales, the library class listens to *The Three Billy Goats Gruff*.

2. After hearing the fairy tale, the class explains plot and characters.

3. Students prepare a goat puppet show using the worksheets to create the puppets.

4. Students color and cut out the goats.

5. Students' goats will be glued or taped onto straws. If students wish to include a troll in the play, they may design their own troll puppet as well.

6. Students may use a chair for a stage, or the art teacher may wish to have students design actual puppet stages during art class.

7. Students may perform their puppet shows for small groups or for other classes during the next library session.

## Learning Styles

Linguistic (telling stories), spatial (coloring and designing), and bodily kinesthetic (acting)

## Teaching Team

Art, language arts, and library teachers

## Suggested Resources

Any version of *The Three Billy Goats Gruff*.

Galdone, Paul. *Three Little Billy Goats Gruff*. New York: Clarion Books, 1984.

Stevens, Janet. *Three Billy Goats Gruff*. San Diego, CA: Harcourt Brace Jovanovich, 1987.

# Presidents

## Standards

Students will

- Demonstrate a basic familiarity with selected works of nonfiction (McREL 11)
- Access information efficiently and effectively (AASL/AECT 1)
- Evaluate information critically and competently (AASL/AECT 2)
- Use information accurately and creatively (AASL/AECT 3)
- Recognize the importance of information to a democratic society (AASL/AECT 7)
- Participate effectively in groups to pursue and generate information (AASL/AECT 9)

## Objectives

Students generate information about George Washington and Abraham Lincoln after listening to the teacher read facts from simple biographies. Students write a simple two- to three-word phrase about each president on presidential portraits. Students create backgrounds for the presidential portraits.

## Directions

1. The library teacher locates easy-reading biography books on Presidents Lincoln and Washington (such as the picture-book biographies by David Adler).
2. The teacher reads brief facts from each biography.
3. Students recite the facts back to the teacher.
4. The teacher writes the facts in simple two- or three-word phrases on the board.
5. For each president, students copy one fact from the board on each presidential portrait on their worksheets.
6. Students cut and glue the presidents onto either red paper squares or red paper valentines for a president background.
7. The social studies teacher may review Lincoln and Washington facts in social studies class following this library lesson.

## Learning Styles

Linguistic (writing), interpersonal (discussing), and spatial (cutting)

## Teaching Team

Library and social studies teachers

## Suggested Resources

Adler, David A. *Picture Book of Abraham Lincoln.* New York: Holiday House, 1989.

Adler, David A. *Picture Book of George Washington.* New York: Holiday House, 1989.

# Butterflies

## Standards

Students will

- Use picture clues and picture captions as an aid to comprehension (McREL 2)
- Demonstrate a basic familiarity with selected works of nonfiction (McREL 11)
- Access information efficiently and effectively (AASL/AECT 1)
- Evaluate information critically and competently (AASL/AECT 2)
- Use information accurately and creatively (AASL/AECT 3)
- Pursue information related to personal interest (AASL/AECT 4)
- Practice ethical behavior in regard to information and information technology (AASL/AECT 8)

## Objectives

Students listen to and then discuss butterfly facts. Students locate information about different kinds of butterflies. Students color and create butterfly kites.

## Directions

1. The library teacher copies the butterfly worksheets (using heavier paper if the students will be making kites).

2. The teacher reads and discusses parts of easy-reading nonfiction books about butterflies (for example, *Butterfly* by Mary Ling or *Butterfly Alphabet Book* by Brian Cassie). They may use an encyclopedia if resources are limited.

3. The teacher shows colorful butterfly pictures or illustrations from nonfiction sources. (The teacher could also have the *Butterflies* CD-ROM computer program running to show more colorful butterflies. *World Book Encyclopedia* has many colorful butterfly varieties.) Students find a colorful butterfly picture to use as a sample for their worksheets.

4. Students design and color a butterfly on their worksheets.

5. In art class, students can turn the butterfly sheets into kites by stapling a 12-inch-long ribbon to their butterflies. Then students can let their butterflies fly in art class.

6. If there is sufficient time, the library or art teacher may read *The Very Hungry Caterpillar* by Eric Carle.

7. The science teacher may wish to follow up this lesson with a unit on butterflies or insects.

## Learning Styles

Linguistic (reading), spatial (creating), bodily kinesthetic (being active), interpersonal learners (group work), and intrapersonal learner (working alone)

## Teaching Team

Art, library, and science teachers

## Suggested Resources

*Butterflies*. Washington, DC: National Geographic, 1993 [CD-ROM].

"Butterflies." *World Book Encyclopedia*. Chicago: World Book, 2001.

Carle, Eric. *The Very Hungry Caterpillar*. New York: Philomel Books, 1994.

Cassie, Brian, and Jerry Pallotta. *Butterfly Alphabet*. Watertown, MA: Charlesbridge, 1995.

Ling, Mary. *Butterfly*. New York: Dorling Kindersley, 1992.

## Here Comes Peter Rabbit!

_____

_____

_____

_____

## Standards

Students will

- Demonstrate knowledge of the plots and major characters of selected classic fairy tales, folktales, legends, and fables from around the world (McREL 9)

- Demonstrate a familiarity with selected fiction and poetry (McREL 10)

- Appreciate literature and other creative expressions (AASL/AECT 5)

## Objectives

Students listen as the Peter Rabbit tale is read aloud. Students discuss the main plot and characters. The class will compose a Peter Rabbit poem.

## Directions

1. The library teacher reads *The Tale of Peter Rabbit*. (This may be a good lesson for Easter or springtime.)

2. Students discuss the plot and characters.

3. The teacher helps the class think of a short rhyming poem to fit the plot of Peter Rabbit. If there isn't time for the class to compose a poem, they may use the following:

Hop, hop!
In the garden spot.
In the water can. Plop!
Hip! Hop! Hop!

4. The teacher writes the poem on the board for students to copy. The teacher may also photocopy the poem for the students.

5. Students write or glue their poems on their rabbit worksheets.

6. Students color the worksheets.

7. In language arts class, students can share their poems and then view the Peter Rabbit story on video.

## Learning Styles

Linguistic (writing), musical (rhythm of poetry), interpersonal (working in groups), and spatial (coloring)

## Teaching Team

Language arts and library teachers

## Suggested Resources

Potter, Beatrice. *The Tale of Peter Rabbit*. New York: Grosset & Dunlap, 1986.

*The Tale of Peter Rabbit*. New York: Ambrose, 1991 [video].

_____

**Hoot! Hoot!**

# Standards

Students will

- Use picture clues and picture captions as an aid to comprehension (McREL 2)
- Demonstrate a familiarity with selected works of fiction and poetry (McREL 10)
- Demonstrate a familiarity with selected works of nonfiction (McREL 11)
- Access information efficiently and effectively (AASL/AECT 1)
- Evaluate information critically and competently (AASL/AECT 2)

# Objectives

Students learn that encyclopedias include information about many topics, including owls. Students describe some brief owl facts as acquired from the encyclopedia discussion. Students create owl masks. Students may pretend to be owls and act out according to the fictional books.

# Directions

1. This lesson provides an introduction to using an encyclopedia. The library teacher points out that there are a lot of books or volumes in an encyclopedia set. The teacher explains that the class will use the "O" encyclopedia for this lesson.

2. The teacher reads three to four facts about owls from the encyclopedia. The teacher also reads the encyclopedia photo captions to show students that captions contain information.

3. The teacher asks students what new things they have learned about owls.

4. Then students color the owl masks on the owl worksheets. The art teacher may wish to teach this part of this lesson.

5. The eyes of the owl masks should be cut out so that students can see. (Teachers may have to do this ahead of time.)

6. The teacher then reads an owl fiction book. (One example is *Owly* by Mike Thaler.) The class pretends to be owls with their owl masks.

# Learning Styles

Spatial (coloring), interpersonal (discussing), intrapersonal (individual work), and bodily kinesthetic (acting)

# Teaching Team

Art and library teachers

# Suggested Resources

"Owls." *World Book Encyclopedia*. Chicago: World Book, 2001.

Thaler, Mike. *Owly*. New York: Walker & Company, 1998.

## Three Pigs

## Standards

Students will

- Use pictures clues and picture captions as an aid to comprehension (McREL 2)
- Comprehend the basic plot of simple stories (McREL 3)
- Identify the main characters in works containing only a few basic characters (McREL 7)
- When prompted by the teacher, recite the texts of a variety of familiar rhymes (McREL 8)
- Appreciate literature and other creative expressions (AASL/AECT 5)

## Objectives

Students discuss the plot and characters of *The Three Little Pigs* fairy tale. Students recite rhymes from the fairy tale. Students hear another version of the tale. Students create their own versions of the fairy tale and design puppets.

## Directions

1. As the library teacher shows students pictures from the familiar story of *The Three Little Pigs*, the class tells the story. While helping to tell the story, the class will have fun reciting the familiar rhyme of "Little Pig, Little Pig, Let me come in. Not by the hair of my chinny, chin chin."

2. Following the storytelling, the class discusses plot and characters.

3. The teacher reads a different version of *The Three Little Pigs* (such as *The True Story of the Three Little Pigs* by John Scieszka).

4. The class tells the plot and characters of that version of the story.

5. Students will think of their own version of the tale. To gather ideas for a different version, students may view *The Three Little Pigs* CD-ROM.

6. During art class, students may create puppets of the three pigs. They may finish designing the three pigs and a wolf character on the worksheet. Their puppets can be taped on straws for the puppet shows.

## Learning Styles

Linguistic (telling a story), intrapersonal (working alone), spatial (coloring), and bodily kinesthetic (acting)

## Teaching Team

Art and library teachers

## Suggested Resources

Galdone, Paul. *The Three Little Pigs*. New York: Clarion Books, 1970.

Kellogg, Steven. *The Three Little Pigs*. New York: William Morrow, 1997.

Miles. Betty. *Three Little Pigs*. New York: Aladdin, 1998.

Scieszka, Jon. *The True Story of the Three Little Pigs*. New York: Viking Kestrel, 1989.

*The Three Little Pigs*. Chicago: Churchill, 1991 [CD-ROM].

# Spiders

# Standards

Students will

- Understand reading is a way of gaining information about the world (McREL 1)
- Demonstrate a basic familiarity with selected works of nonfiction (McREL 11)
- Access information efficiently and effectively (AASL/AECT 1)
- Evaluate information critically and competently (AASL/AECT 2)
- Use information accurately and creatively (AASL/AECT 3)
- Strive for excellence in information seeking (ASL/AECT 6)

# Objectives

Students discover facts about spiders. Students write down simple spider facts around a spider web worksheet.

# Directions

1. The library teacher collects easy-reading nonfiction books about spiders. (Two examples are *Spider* by Michael Chinery and *Spiders* by Janet Resnick. The encyclopedia could provide another resource.)

2. The teacher reads or tells the students brief facts about spiders from the nonfiction sources. Facts could include information about their size, what they eat, where they live, and which types are poisonous.

3. The class repeats the facts, which the teacher writes on the board. An example would be, "Spiders have 8 legs."

4. The class copies one or two of these facts around the spider web on the worksheets.

5. Some students may want to find more facts by looking through the sources. Others may prefer just to browse through the sources.

6. In science class, students may wish to unearth more facts about spiders or other insects.

7. Students may wish to sing and act out the "Itsy Bitsy Spider" rhyming song in music class.

# Learning Styles

Linguistic (writing), bodily kinesthetic (acting), and musical (singing)

# Teaching Team

Library, music, and science teachers

# Suggested Resources

Chinery, Michael. *Spider*. Mahwah, NJ: Troll, 1991.

Resnick, Janet. *Spiders*. Chicago: Kidsbooks, 1996.

"Spiders." *World Book Encyclopedia*. Chicago: World Book, 2001 [CD-ROM].

Trapani, Iza. *Itsy Bitsy Spider*. Boston: Whispering Coyote Press, 1993.

# I Know I Can. Choo! Choo!

I know I can. Choo! Choo!

## Standards

Students will

- Make simple inferences regarding "what will happen next" or "how things could have turned out differently" (McREL 4)
- Demonstrate a basic familiarity with selected fiction and poetry (McREL 10)
- Appreciate literature and other creative expressions (AASL/AECT 5)

## Objectives

Students discuss and define characters from "The Little Engine That Could." Students infer different parts of the story. Students color train bookmarks.

## Directions

1. The library teacher makes several copies of the train included with this lesson plan.
2. The teacher reads *The Little Engine That Could*. While reading the book, the teacher stops occasionally to ask what will happen next.
3. The teacher will discuss the characters of the story, while examining the main character of the Little Engine most carefully.
4. Students color the trains on their worksheets.
5. Students will cut out the train bookmarks, which serve as student reminders that they should try to work hard.
6. The music or library teacher may show the book in video format for a follow-up.

## Learning Styles

Spatial (drawing and coloring), linguistic (discussing), and intrapersonal learners (working alone)

## Teaching Team

Music and library teachers

## Suggested Resources

*The Little Engine That Could*. Phoenix, AZ: BFA, 1963 [video].

Piper, Watty. *The Little Engine That Could*. New York: Platt & Monk, 1976.

## My Favorite Fiction

My favorite book:

Title: _____

_____

Author: _____

My favorite part:

## Standards

Students will

- Demonstrate a basic familiarity with selected fiction and poetry (McREL 10)
- Share responses to literature with peers (McREL 6)
- Appreciate literature and other creative expressions (AASL/AECT 5)

## Objectives

Students read and compare favorite fiction books. Students write down the title and author of their favorite books. Students illustrate their favorite part of their books.

## Directions

1. This lesson works best in the spring, when first-graders have improved their reading skills. The library teacher selects a favorite fiction book. (An example is *Edward and the Pirates* by David McPhail.) After choosing a favorite book, the teacher writes down the title and author on the board.

2. The teacher reads the book to the class, pointing out a favorite part.

3. Students find a favorite fiction book of their own.

4. The teacher shows students how to write down the title and author of their books on the worksheets.

5. Students illustrate their favorite part of the books on their worksheets.

6. Students will share their worksheets with the class, so that others may become familiar with other fiction books mentioned on the sheets.

7. For a reinforcement, the language arts teacher may share a favorite fiction book, discuss the title and author, and then read and discuss it in English class.

## Learning Styles

Linguistic (reading), intrapersonal (working alone), and spatial (drawing)

## Teaching Team

Language arts and library teachers

## Suggested Resources

McPhail, David M. *Edward and the Pirates*. Boston: Little, Brown, 1997.

# Frog's Story

## Standards

Students will

- Make simple inferences regarding "what will happen next" or "how things could have turned out differently" (McREL 4)

- Identify the main characters in works containing only a few basic characters (McREL 7)

- Demonstrate a basic familiarity with selected fiction and poetry (McREL 10)

- Appreciate literature and other creative expressions (AASL/AECT 5)

## Objectives

Students discuss the characters from the Frog and Toad books. Students listen to a chapter from one of the books. Students suggest and then illustrate a different ending for the story. Students color their worksheets.

## Directions

1.  The library teacher provides students with the frog sheets.

2.  The library teacher reads one or two chapters out of the easy-reading chapter books from Lobel's Frog and Toad books. (Examples are *Frog and Toad Are Friends* or *Frog and Toad All Year.*)

3.  The class talks about the two main characters, Frog and Toad.

4.  Then the class will see if they can come up with a different ending for one of the stories.

5.  Students can illustrate their different ending on their frog worksheets.

6.  Students color their worksheets.

7.  Students may enjoy watching the video format of the Frog and Toad books during the next library time.

8.  The language arts teacher may wish to continue the Lobel author study by sharing more of the Frog and Toad books.

## Learning Styles

Linguistic (writing and discussing), intrapersonal (working alone), and spatial (coloring)

## Teaching Team

Language arts and library teachers

## Suggested Resources

*Frog and Toad Are Friends*. Chicago: Churchill, 1985 [video].

Lobel, Arnold. *Frog and Toad All Year*. New York: Harper & Row, 1976.

Lobel, Arnold. *Frog and Toad Are Friends*. New York: Harper & Row, 1970.

# Chapter 3

## Second-Grade Lesson Plans

In order to create solid professional-based library lesson plans, the following selected Kendall and Marzano or McREL National Education Standards and Benchmarks for Kindergarten were chosen from the area of language arts, as it directly correlates with library information and appreciation skills. Furthermore, the AASL (American Association of School Libraries) and the AECT (Association for Educational Communications and Technology) list of Information Literacy Standards were applied to every lesson to ensure that all students will develop literary appreciation and will be effective users of information and ideas (listed in the Introduction). Teaching objectives were also given for each lesson as linked to the standards or active goals. Finally, Gardner's multiple intelligences are also integrated into each lesson, as all students have different methods of learning (also listed in the Introduction).

*Each lesson plan has a direct reference to the following numbered McREL benchmarks under the corresponding standards, as well as a direct reference to AASL/AECT standards.* Finally, all of the following twenty-minute lesson plans should be used in conjunction with the other teachers whenever possible. Moreover, all lesson plans are not the only means, but some of many, for library instruction. The following lessons can provide whole group discussion ideas, or they can provide individual or small group worksheet work.

# Second-Grade Library Standards and Language Arts Benchmarks (McREL)*

Second-grade students will be able to

- Demonstrate competence in the general skills and strategies of the reading process (Standard 5)

    1.  Understand reading is a way of gaining information about the world

    2.  Use picture clues and picture captions as an aid to comprehension

- Demonstrate competence in general skills and strategies for reading literature (Standard 6)

    3.  Comprehend the basic plot of simple stories

    4.  Make simple inferences regarding "what will happen next" or "how things could have turned out differently"

    5.  Become aware of the geographic information important to the stories one reads (for grades 3–5)

    6.  Share responses to literature with peers (for grades 3–5)

    7.  Identify the main characters in works containing only a few basic characters (for grades 3–5)

- Demonstrate competence in the general skills and strategies for reading information (for grades 3–5) (Standard 7)

    8.  Understand the uses of the various parts of a book (index, table of contents, glossary, appendix)

- Demonstrate a familiarity with selected literary works of enduring quality (Standard 13)

    9.  When prompted by the teacher recite the texts of a variety of familiar rhymes

    10.  Demonstrate a knowledge of the plots and major characters of selected classic fairy tales, folktales, legends, and fables from around the world

    11.  Demonstrate a basic familiarity with selected fiction and poetry

    12.  Demonstrate a basic familiarity with selected works of nonfiction

# Flying with Bats

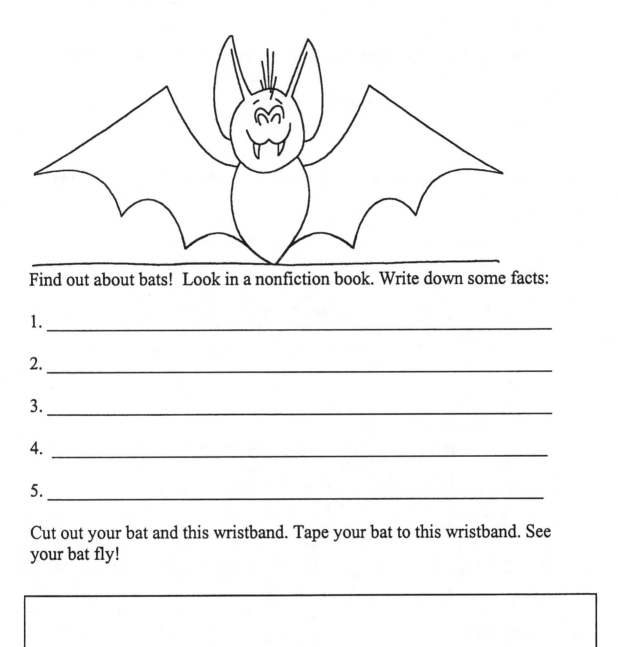

Find out about bats! Look in a nonfiction book. Write down some facts:

1. _____

2. _____

3. _____

4. _____

5. _____

Cut out your bat and this wristband. Tape your bat to this wristband. See your bat fly!

## Standards

Students will

- Understand that reading is a way of gaining information about the world (McREL 1)
- Demonstrate a basic familiarity with selected works of nonfiction (McREL 12)
- Access information efficiently and effectively (AASL/AECT 1)
- Evaluate information critically and competently (AASL/AECT 3)
- Use information accurately and creatively (AASL/AECT 4)
- Participate effectively in groups to pursue and generate information (AASL/AECT 9)

## Objectives

Students acquire four to five facts about bats for the bat worksheet. Students may create bat wristbands.

## Directions

1. The library teacher provides students with a copy of the bat worksheet. This lesson may fit into Halloween or fall activities as given by classroom teachers.
2. The teacher shows students how to locate information on bats in nonfiction books or encyclopedias. If possible, those sources should be set out for easy access. (Some examples of nonfiction bat books are *Bats* by Lynn Stone or *Bats* by Betsy Maestro.)
3. Small groups of students will find four to five bat facts from the nonfiction sources by examining the pictures or text.
4. Small groups of students will find four to five facts about bats from their nonfiction sources.
5. Their bats will then fly! Students may also complete this activity in art class.
6. The language arts teacher may wish to read the fictional bat book titled *Stellaluna*, followed by the video, in order to compare video and print formats.

## Learning Styles

Linguistic (reading and writing), spatial (coloring), and interpersonal (working in groups)

## Teaching Team

Art, language art, and library teachers

## Suggested Resources

Cannon, Janell. *Stellaluna*. San Diego, CA: Harcourt Brace Jovanovich, 1993.

Maestro, Betsy. *Bats*. New York: Scholastic, 1994.

*Stellaluna*. Lincoln, NE: GPN, 1994 [video].

# Legend of the Poinsettia

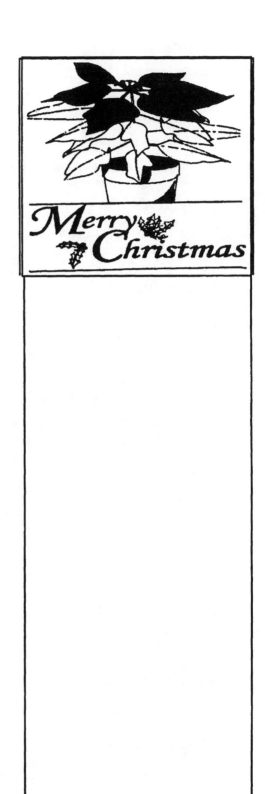

## Standards

Students will

- Demonstrate a knowledge of the plots and major characters of selected classic fairy tales, folktales, legends, and fables from around the world (McREL 10)

- Appreciate literature and other creative expressions (AASL/AECT 5)

- Recognize the importance of information to a democratic society (AASL/AECT 7)

# Objectives

Students discuss plot and characters from *The Legend of the Poinsettia* after listening to it. Students illustrate the plot on bookmarks.

# Directions

1. The library teacher reads Tomie dePaola's book *The Legend of the Poinsettia*. This Christmas story includes some Spanish words.

2. If a Spanish teacher is available, he or she may wish to help with this lesson by having students learn a couple of simple Spanish words or phrases.

3. After hearing the legend, students discuss plot and character.

4. The bookmark sheets should be copied onto construction paper, perhaps using Christmas colors.

5. Students illustrate the plot of the story on one or two of the bookmarks. Then they can decorate the bookmark(s).

6. Students could give the bookmark(s) to someone for a gift, following the example of the little girl in *The Legend of the Poinsettia* who also gave a gift. They may retell the legend to the person who receives their bookmark gift.

7. In language arts class, the teacher may read another legend by dePaola, *The Legend of the Persian Carpet*. Students may discuss the plot and characters from that legend as well.

# Learning Styles

Spatial (drawing and coloring) and linguistic (retelling the story)

# Teaching Team

Language arts, library, and science teachers

# Suggested Resources

dePaola, Tomie. *The Legend of the Persian Carpet*. New York: G. P. Putnam's Sons, 1993.

dePaola, Tomie. *The Legend of the Poinsettia*. New York: G. P. Putnam's Sons, 1994.

## Standards

Students will

- Make simple inferences regarding "what will happen next" or how things could have turned out differently (McREL 4)

- Share responses to literature with peers (McREL 6)

- Demonstrate a knowledge of the plots and major characters of selected classic fairy tales, folktales, legends, and fables from around the world (McREL 10)

- Appreciate literature and other creative expressions (AASL/AECT 5)

## Objectives

Students will create inferences of possible story parts while listening to the folktale of Pecos Bill. After hearing the folktale, students deduce which parts of the folktale were exaggerated. Students discuss character and plot and then illustrate the plot in the lasso of the Pecos Bill worksheet.

## Directions

1. The library teacher locates an easy-reading folktale of Pecos Bill. (Resources include *Pecos Bill* by Steven Kellogg or *Classic American Folk Tales* by Steven Zorn.)

2. The teacher explains to students that folktales are stories with parts that were true. As the folktales were retold a lot of times, the stories became exaggerated. The teacher then tells students to listen to the story of *Pecos Bill* to decide which parts are true.

3. While reading *Pecos Bill*, the teacher stops once in a while to ask students what will happen next.

4. After reading the story, the teacher begins a discussion of plot and character.

5. In the lasso, students will write one or two brief thoughts about the character of Pecos Bill.

6. If there is enough time, students can color Pecos Bill and create a background on the worksheets. Their worksheets can then be displayed.

7. If students complete their worksheets early, they may access the *Pecos Bill* CD-ROM.

8. In language arts class, students may read and discuss other folktales from books such as *Classic American Folk Tales* by Steven Zorn.

## Learning Styles

Linguistic (writing) and spatial (coloring)

## Teaching Team

Language arts and library teachers

## Suggested Resources

Kellogg, Steven. *Pecos Bill*. New York: William Morrow, 1986.

*Pecos Bill*. Toronto, Canada: Harmony Interactive Discs Distributors, 1996 [CD-ROM].

Zorn, Steven. *Classic American Folk Tales*. Philadelphia: Running Press, 1992.

## Ugly Duckling

Help the Ugly Duckling find his way home through the water.

What made the duckling happy?

## Standards

Students will

- Make simple inferences regarding "what will happen next" or "how things could have turned out differently" (McREL 4)

- Demonstrate a knowledge of plots and major characters of selected classic fairy tales, folktales, legends, and fables from around the world (McREL 10)

- Appreciate literature and other creative expressions (AASL/AECT 5)

## Objectives

Students discuss the main plot and possible inferences after hearing *The Ugly Duckling* fairy tale. Students complete duckling worksheets by writing about what made the duckling feel better and by completing the water maze.

## Directions

1. The library teacher tells or reads most, but not all, of the classic fairy tale, *The Ugly Duckling*, as it is quite lengthy. (*The Ugly Duckling* as retold by Lillian Moore has been nicely illustrated by Robert San Souci.)

2. Once the tale has been read, students will discuss the main character and plot and then decide "how things could have turned out differently."

3. Students are ready to complete the duckling worksheet. They will draw the ducklings' trip through the water maze and then write what made the duckling feel better (he realized how wonderful he really was).

4. Students can color their worksheets.

5. The language arts teacher may wish to expand on this lesson by showing *The Ugly Duckling* video.

## Learning Styles

Linguistic (writing), intrapersonal (working alone), and spatial (puzzles and coloring)

## Teaching Team

Language arts and library teachers

## Suggested Resources

Any version of *The Ugly Duckling*.

Anderson, Hans, and Jerry Pinkney. *The Ugly Duckling*. New York: Morrow, 1999.

*Ugly Duckling*. Phoenix, AZ: BFA, 1980 [video].

## What Should You Do?

The sheep would say to tell the truth.

The sheep would say to tell the truth.

**What should you do?**
**Do you want to have a play?**

## THE PLAY OF THE SHEPHERD BOY AND THE WOLF.

*Actors:* The boy, the wolf, and three or four town people.

*Scene I*
The boy pretends to take care of imaginary sheep. He could feed them, or...
Then the boy acts like he is thinking of a silly idea. He jumps up!
The boy yells: "Wolf, wolf"...
The town people are working at imaginary jobs, like sweeping or cleaning...
When the people hear the boy, they stop working. They hurry to help.
When the town people get to the boy, they stop and look puzzled.
Then they act mad. So, they leave!

*Scene II*
The boy should pretend to think of the silly idea again.
The boy yells: "Wolf, wolf."
The town people are once again working.
The town people hear the boy yelling and hurry to help again.
However, when the town people get there, they are really disgusted!
The people leave even angrier than before.

*Scene III*
Finally, the character of the wolf comes growling up and pretends to eat up
imaginary sheep.
The boy yells, "Wolf, wolf."
But, the town people ignore him.
The boy looks sad. He slowly walks away.

**The End!  Applause!**

## Standards

Students will

- Make simple inferences regarding "what will happen next" or "how things could have turned out differently" (McREL 4)

- Share responses to literature with peers (McREL 6)

- Demonstrate a knowledge of the plots and major characters of selected classic fairy tales, folktales, legends, and fable from around the world (McREL 10)

- Appreciate literature and other creative expressions (AASL/AECT 5)

- Recognize the importance of information to a democratic society (AASL/AECT 7)

- Participate effectively in groups to pursue and generate information (AASL/AECT 9)

## Objectives

After hearing "The Shepherd Boy and the Wolf" fable, students will discuss the plot and main character. They will act out the fable. Students will color a bookmark.

## Directions

1. The library teacher reads "The Shepherd Boy and the Wolf." This story can be found in most fable books, including *The Aseop for Children* as retold by Milo Winter.

2. The class will discuss what the story is all about (the plot), the main character, and how the characters could have done things differently.

3. The teacher helps the class act out this story from the play worksheet. The teacher will read the play from the worksheet as students act it out.

4. Students can color the bookmark on the bottom of this sheet as a reminder of the fable.

5. As a follow-up in library class or in language arts class, students may access the *Aesop's Fables* CD-ROM.

## Learning Styles

Linguistic (reading), spatial (coloring), and bodily kinesthetic (acting)

## Teaching Team

Language arts and library teachers

## Suggested Resources

Any version of Aesop's fables.

*Aesop's Fables*. New York: Discis, 1993 [CD-ROM].

Winter, Milo. *The Aesop for Children*. New York: Barnes & Noble, 1993.

# Pieces of Great Caldecott Books

## Standards

Students will

- Demonstrate a basic familiarity with selected fiction and poetry (McREL 11)
- Appreciate literature and other creative expressions (AASL/AECT 5)

## Objectives

Students become aware of books that have won the Caldecott Medal. Students will illustrate a Caldecott book while listening to the book. Students make puzzles from their illustrations.

## Directions

1.  The library teacher locates selections of Caldecott Medal–winning books for the class.
2.  The teacher makes copies of the Caldecott puzzle worksheet from card stock. The art teacher may wish to help students create the Caldecott puzzles from the worksheets.
3.  The library teacher should tell students that Caldecott books are given medals because their illustrations or pictures are the best. The teacher should show some illustrations of three or four of the Caldecott books. (Some Caldecott titles are listed in the Suggested Resources section.)
4.  The library teacher reads a Caldecott book, such as *Hey Al*. As students listen, they colorfully illustrate any part of the story on their puzzle worksheets, without having seen any of the actual illustrations. When they are done illustrating, students will have a Caldecott puzzle.
5.  If there is time, students can share their puzzle illustrations.
6.  As a library follow-up, students may view Caldecott books on video (such as *Officer Buckle and Gloria* or *Zin! Zin! Zin! A Violin!*).

## Learning Styles

Spatial (drawing and coloring) and intrapersonal (working alone)

## Teaching Team

Art and library teachers

## Suggested Resources

Teachers can find a list of Caldecott Medal winners at http://www.ala.org/alsc/caldecott.html. The following are examples:

Ackerman, Karen. *Song and Dance Man*. New York: Knopf, 1988.

Eberley, Barbara. *Drummer Hoff*. Englewood Cliffs, NJ: Prentice-Hall, 1967.

Hader, Berta, and Elmer Hader. *The Big Snow*. New York: Macmillan, 1976.

Lionni, Leo. *Frederick*. New York: Pantheon Books, 1967.

McCloskey, Robert. *Make Way for Ducklings*. New York: Viking, 1941.

McCully, Emily Arnold. *Mirette on the Highwire*. New York: Putnam, 1992.

*Officer Buckle and Gloria.* Westport, CT: Weston Woods, 1998 [video].

Rothmann, Peggy. *Officer Buckle and Gloria.* New York: Putnam, 1995.

Sendak, Maurice. *Where the Wild Things Are.* New York: Harper & Row, 1963.

Van Allsburg, Chris. *Jumanji.* Boston: Houghton Mifflin, 1981.

Ward, Lynd. *The Biggest Bear.* Boston: Houghton Mifflin, 1980.

Weisner, David. *Tuesday.* New York: Clarion Books, 1961.

Williams, Shereley, Anne. *Working Cotton.* San Diego, CA: Harcourt Brace & Jovanovich.

Wood, Audrey. *King Bidgood Is in the Bathtub.* San Diego, CA: Harcourt Brace & Jovanovich.

Yorinks, Arthur. *Hey Al.* New York: Farrar, Straus & Giroux, 1986.

*Zin ! Zin! Zin! A Violin!* Lincoln, NE: Reading Rainbow Series, 1995 [video].

## SSS . . . Snakes

What do you know about snakes? Write the facts around this snake.

## Standards

Students will

- Understand reading is a way of gaining information about the world (McREL 1)
- Use picture clues and picture captions as an aid to comprehension (McREL 2)
- Access information efficiently and effectively (AASL/AECT 1)
- Evaluate information critically and competently (AASL/AECT 2)
- Use information accurately and creatively (AASL/AECT 3)
- Strive for excellence in information seeking (AASL/AECT 6)
- Practice ethical behavior in regard to information and information technology (AASL/AECT 8)
- Participate effectively in groups to pursue and generate information (AASL/AECT 9)

## Objectives

Students discover some simple facts about snakes from pictures of snakes in the encyclopedia. Students write their facts around snakes on the worksheets.

## Directions

1. Using encyclopedias, students research simple facts about snakes. The library teacher may want to gather extra encyclopedia volumes for this lesson. (*World Book Encyclopedia* would be a good resource for this age level.)

2. The teacher shows and tells students how to find the correct encyclopedia volumes. The teacher shows students that pictures in encyclopedias have captions that provide additional information.

3. Small groups of students will find some information about snakes by reading the picture captions in the encyclopedia, or by simply looking at the pictures.

4. Students will write one or two snake facts around the snakes on the worksheets. They may also color their snakes.

5. If there is time, groups can share their information in library or science class.

6. The science teacher may have students search a simple CD-ROM encyclopedia (such as *First Connections: The Golden Book Encyclopedia*) for more snake facts to share in science class.

## Learning Styles

Linguistic (reading and writing), spatial (coloring), and interpersonal (group work)

## Teaching Team

Library and science teachers

## Suggested Resources

"S" volumes of children's encyclopedias.

*First Connections: The Golden Book Encyclopedia.* San Diego, CA: Josten's Learning, 1992 [CD-ROM].

# The Wolf

1. Who will be in your story? _____

_____

2. Where will your story take place? _____

3. What will happen in your story? _____

_____

_____

_____

_____

## Standards

Students will

- Become aware of the geographic information important to the stories one reads (McREL 5)
- Demonstrate a knowledge of the plots and major characters of selected classic fairy tales, folktales, legends, and fables from around the world (McREL 10)
- Appreciate literature and other creative expressions (AASL/AECT 5)
- Participate effectively in groups to pursue and generate information (AASL/AECT 9)

## Objectives

Students review *Little Red Riding Hood*. Students will listen to another version of the story and then compare it with the original. The class creates their own version of *Little Red Riding Hood*.

## Directions

1. The library teacher makes an overhead transparency of the wolf sheet.
2. The class orally reviews what they recall about the classic fairy tale, *Little Red Riding Hood*. The teacher may show pictures of Little Red Riding Hood from a well-known version to spark the review.
3. The teacher reads another version, such as *Lon Po Po: A Red Riding Hood Story from China*.
4. The class writes their own version of *Little Red Riding Hood*, after brainstorming ideas.
5. The teacher writes the story on the overhead transparency.
6. In art class, students can turn their story into a children's picture book. Each student may be assigned a different part of the story to be illustrated on 8 x 11 sheets for their children's picture book. The class-illustrated version of *Little Red Riding Hood* may be duplicated and a copy of it given to the school library media center. Another copy can be placed in the classroom. The book may also be illustrated and written by students using the computer program called *EasyBook Deluxe*.
7. The language arts teacher may have students discuss another version of *Little Red Riding Hood* in English class.

## Learning Styles

Linguistic (writing), interpersonal (group work), intrapersonal (working alone), and spatial (illustrating)

## Teaching Team

Art, language arts, and library teachers

## Suggested Resources

*EasyBook Deluxe*. New York: Sunburst Technology, 2000 [CD-ROM].

Hyman, Trina. *Little Red Riding Hood*. New York: Holiday House, 1983.

Young, Ed. *Lon Po Po: A Red Riding Hood Story from China*. New York: Econo-Clad Books, 1999.

# What Does "Valentine" Mean?

    Think of a word that you would put on a Valentine card. Put that word on one heart.

    Look up that word in the dictionary. Put the definition for the word on the other heart.

## Standards

Students will

- Demonstrate a basic familiarity with selected works of fiction and poetry (McREL 11)
- Demonstrate a basic familiarity with selected works of nonfiction (McREL 12)
- Access information efficiently and effectively (AASL/AECT 1)
- Evaluate information critically and competently (AASL/AECT 2)
- Use information accurately and creatively (AASL/AECT 3)
- Participate effectively in groups to pursue and generate information (AASL/AECT 9)

## Objectives

Students learn how to use dictionaries by locating a word associated with valentines. Students write down the word and then the definition on valentine hearts. Students decorate their hearts.

## Directions

1. Students learn how to use a children's dictionary. A good dictionary for this age group would be *My First Dictionary*. There should be multiple dictionary copies collected and available for small-group work.

2. The teacher makes copies of the valentine worksheets on pink or red paper.

3. The teacher shows students how to use a dictionary. For an introduction, students think of a couple of words to look up in the dictionary.

4. The class should think of words that would be found both in a dictionary and on a valentine greeting card. (Examples are *love, kind, friend, good, like, sweet,* or *hug.*) The teacher lists the examples on the board.

5. Students choose a word from the list, write it down on the left worksheet heart, and follow it with an equal sign.

6. On the other heart, students write down a simple definition of the word after they have looked it up. (For example, like = love.)

7. Students decorate the hearts and then give them away. The art teacher may have the students decorate the hearts in art class.

8. Students could listen to a Valentine's Day fiction book such as *One Zillion Valentines, Super-Fine Valentine,* or *Nate the Great and the Mushy Valentine* in language arts class.

## Learning Styles

Linguistic (reading) and bodily kinesthetic (crafts)

## Teaching Team

Art, language art, and library teachers

## Suggested Resources

A children's dictionary.

Cosby, Bill. *Super Fine Valentine*. New York: Scholastic, 1998.

Modell, Frank. *One Zillion Valentines*. New York: Econo-Clad Books, 1999.

Sharmat, Marjorie Weinman. *Nate the Great and the Mushy Valentine*. New York: Delacorte Press, 1994.

# Henny Penny and Friends

Henny Penny

Foxey Loxey

Ducky Lucky

Cockey Lockey

Turkey Lurkey

Goosey Loosey

## Standards

Students will

- Share responses to literature with peers (McREL 6)
- Demonstrate a knowledge of the plots and characters of selected classic fairy tales, folktales, and fables from around the world (McREL 10)
- Appreciate literature and other creative expressions (AASL/AECT 5)

# Objectives

Students discuss main characters and plot of the *Henny Penny* fairy tale after hearing the story. Students create puppets and act out the fairy tale.

# Directions

1. The library teacher will read the *Henny Penny* fairy tale.
2. After reading the story, the teacher asks the class to name and explain the main characters. Perhaps the teacher could make an overhead of the Henny Penny worksheets to show the class each animal's character and name.
3. The class will discuss what the book was all about (the main plot).
4. Students cut out the animal puppets from the Henny Penny worksheet. These puppets were designed for shadow puppetry but can be used in any way.
5. In art class, students may glue or tape the animal puppets on Popsicle sticks or on straws. Students may take turns telling the story to each other using their puppets.

## Learning Styles

Linguistic (hearing the story) and bodily kinesthetic (acting)

## Teaching Teams

Art and library teachers

## Suggested Resources

Galdone, Paul. *Henny Penny*. New York: Clarion Books, 1968.

# The Color of Book Parts

1. Draw a red line under the author on the cover.

2. Circle the title of the book in blue on the cover.

3. Draw a blue line under the title on the spine.

4. Circle the call number in red.

---

_____
(title)

Fic

_____
(author)

Now, make your own book:

1. Write your title on your book cover.

2. Write your name as the author on your book cover.

3. Illustrate your book cover in bright colors.

## Standards

Students will

- Understand the uses of various parts of a book (index, table of contents, glossary, appendix) (McREL 8)

- Access information efficiently and effectively (AASL/AECT 1)

## Objectives

Students identify book parts. Students devise a title for an imaginary book and then illustrate their book. Students may write a brief story.

## Directions

1. After the language arts teacher has covered book parts in English class, the library teacher will want to follow-up with a book parts lesson.

2. Using several books for examples, the teacher will show students the cover and spine book parts.

3. The teacher shows how a book's cover has the title and author. Likewise, the teacher explains that the book's spine has the title and author on the white tag (or call number). Students learn that the title is on both the spine and the cover.

4. Student volunteers may help by showing the book parts of the cover and spine of two or three books.

5. Once students understand the basics of the cover and spine, they may begin working on the book parts worksheet. Students will need a blue and a red crayon. For the top half of the worksheet, the teacher reads each worksheet question as students circle or draw with the appropriate crayon.

6. After students have answered the top part of the worksheets, the library teacher points out that the title of the book is repeated on the cover and on the spine. Students have underlined the title in blue, so the blue color should provide another visual clue for title recognition.

7. Students will make up a title for an original story and write their name as the book's author. Then they will illustrate the book's cover.

8. The language arts teacher may have students write their original stories during English class.

## Learning Styles

Linguistic (writing), intrapersonal (working alone), and spatial (drawing and coloring)

## Teaching Team

Language arts and library teachers

## Suggested Resources

Any books.

# Driving Through the Index

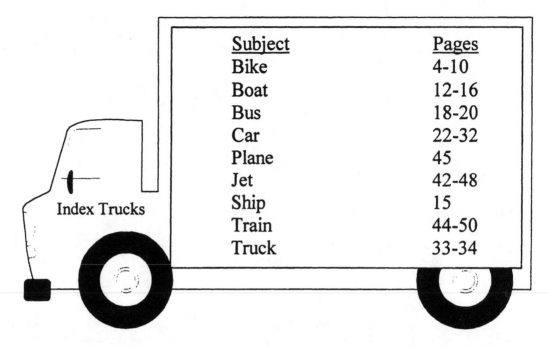

Index Trucks

| Subject | Pages |
|---------|-------|
| Bike | 4-10 |
| Boat | 12-16 |
| Bus | 18-20 |
| Car | 22-32 |
| Plane | 45 |
| Jet | 42-48 |
| Ship | 15 |
| Train | 44-50 |
| Truck | 33-34 |

An index will help you find things.  Read the index above.  Fill in the blanks.

1.  Where would you find something on a Jet?_____

2.  Where could you find the Monorail Train? _____

3.  Which pages have Cars? _____

4.  On what pages are Boats? _____

5.  Where is something on Planes? _____

6.  Where would you find pages on the School Bus? _____

7.  Which subjects would you like to look up?_____

## Standards

Students will

- Understand the uses of various parts of a book (index, table of contents, glossary, appendix) (McREL 8)
- Access information efficiently and effectively (AASL/AECT 1)
- Use information accurately and creatively (AASL/AECT 3)
- Strive for excellence in information seeking (AASL/AECT 6)

## Objectives

Students locate pages from worksheet indexes. Students will locate items of interest by browsing actual indexes.

## Directions

1. The library teacher shows students where to find the indexes in various easy-reading non-fiction books. The teacher displays books for student browsing.

2. The teacher explains the purposes of indexes. He or she provides some index-searching examples by looking up a few things in book indexes. To spark interest, the teacher selects topics of interest to this age group.

3. When students are ready, they fill out the index worksheet. They will need to check their own worksheets and correct any possible errors.

4. Once the students have completed their worksheets, small groups will browse the indexes of various easy-reading nonfiction library books to find topics of interest. They will look up those topics to find interesting facts or pictures for class discussion.

5. Groups share what they have found using indexes.

6. This lesson is a good introduction or review of indexes for the language arts classroom. The language arts teacher may want to follow-up by having students use an index in language arts class.

## Learning Styles

Linguistic (reading and writing) and interpersonal (group work)

## Teaching Team

Language arts and library teachers

## Suggested Resources

The library nonfiction shelves.

## My Monkey Story

Choose a new hat for your monkey. What will your monkey do with the new hat? Write a story to make a folding storybook.

Cut out the story strips. Glue the ends together. Fold on the dotted lines.

## Standards

Students will

- Comprehend the basic plot of simple stories (McREL 3)
- Make simple inferences regarding "what will happen next" or "how things could have turned out differently" (McREL 4)
- Demonstrate a basic familiarity with selected fiction and poetry (McREL 11)
- Demonstrate a basic familiarity with selected works of nonfiction (McREL 12)
- Appreciate literature and other creative expressions (AASL/AECT 5)

## Objectives

Students discuss plot and characters from the *Caps for Sale* story. Students create a picture story booklet of the monkey characters with different hats.

## Directions

1. The language arts teacher can introduce this lesson by reading *Three Hat Day* or *Hats, Hats, Hats* in English class.
2. In library class, the library teacher reads *Caps for Sale* by Esphyr Slobodkina.
3. Students discuss what happened in the *Caps for Sale* story. They should also discuss the characters of the monkeys in the story.
4. The teacher provides students with the monkey worksheets. Students choose and circle a new hat for the monkeys.
5. Students illustrate what they think happened to the monkeys once a different hat was selected. For example, when the monkeys tried on the baker's hat, did they make pies?
6. Students make a folding story picture booklet. They will illustrate their story on each story strip, glue the strips on the solid lines, and then fold on the dotted lines.
7. In language arts class, students may write simple sentences with their pictures and then share their picture booklets.
8. As a follow-up, the language arts or library teacher may show *The Three Hat Day* video.

## Learning Styles

Linguistic (discussing), intrapersonal (working alone), and spatial (imagine and draw)

## Teaching Team

Language arts and library teachers

## Suggested Resources

Geringer, Laura. *Three Hat Day*. New York: Econo-Clad Books, 1999.

Morris, Ann. Ken Heyman, photographer. *Hats, Hats, Hats*. New York: Mulberry Books, 1993.

Slobodkina, Esphyr. *Caps for Sale: A Tale of a Peddler, Some Monkeys, and Their Monkey Business*. New York: HarperCollins Children's Books, 1968.

*Three Hat Day*. Lincoln, NE: Reading Rainbow, 1991 [video].

## The Rabbit

## Standards

Students will

- Demonstrate a basic familiarity with selected fiction and poetry (McREL 11)
- Appreciate literature and other creative expressions (AASL/AECT 5)

## Objectives

Students hear a fictional story about rabbits. Students think of rhyming words to create a couplet poem on rabbits. Students write their poems on rabbit worksheets.

## Directions

1. The library teacher reads a fictional book about rabbits (such as *Happy Easter Day* by Wendy Watson or *The Easter Egg Artists* by Adrienne Adams).

2. After hearing the fiction book, each student creates a couplet rabbit poem for Easter or spring. The teacher explains that a couplet poem is one that has two rhyming lines, such as

   The rabbit went hop, hop, hop.
   Its ears went flop, flop, flop.

3. First, students brainstorm words that are associated with rabbits.

4. Then, students will think of some rhyming words using those facts.

5. As the class composes their two-line poems, the teacher writes the class poem on the board.

6. Students will copy their poems on the two-dotted worksheet lines. In language arts or a later library class, students also could type their poems using a program such as Student Writing Center. They could glue their typed poems on their worksheets.

7. In art or library class, students color the rabbits on their worksheets. The rabbits can be cut out and displayed. (Note that the rabbits can be self-standing if they are folded on the small rectangular box.)

## Learning Styles

Linguistic (writing), musical (rhythm of poetry), mathematical (computers), and spatial (coloring)

## Teaching Team

Art, language art, and library teachers

## Suggested Resources

Fiction books about rabbits.

Adams, Adrienne. *The Easter Egg Artists*. New York: Atheneum, 1976.

*Student Writing Center*. Novato, CA: The Learning Company, 2000 [CD-ROM].

Watson, Wendy. *Happy Easter Day*. New York: Clarion Books, 1993.

# What Will Be Your Pet?

If you could have any pet, what kind of animal would you choose?

_____

Find three facts about your pet in a true (nonfiction) book:

1. _____

2. _____

3. _____

Here is your pet:

```

```

What is your pet's name? _____

## Standards

Students will

- Understand reading is a way of gaining information about the world (McREL 1)
- Demonstrate a basic familiarity with selected works of nonfiction (McREL 12)
- Access information efficiently and effectively (AASL/AECT 1)
- Evaluate information critically and competently (AASL/AECT 2)
- Use information accurately and creatively (AASL/AECT 3)
- Pursue information related to personal interest (AASL/AECT 4)
- Practice ethical behavior in regard to information and information technology (AASL/AECT 8)

## Objectives

Students research an animal that they have chosen as an imaginary pet. Students write three facts about their animal on their pet worksheets. Students draw and then name their pet.

## Directions

1. The library teacher asks students to brainstorm animals that they think would make a good pet. Students may think of some fictitious pet animals, such as dinosaurs.

2. The teacher asks students to find information in nonfiction books about an animal that is not normally considered a pet. Since students need help finding such sources, the teacher will need to either display nonfiction books or show the location of those books.

3. Students write their chosen pet's name of their pet worksheets.

4. Students find three facts about their animals from pictures or text in the nonfiction books. Remind students that they can't copy facts directly from the book. The science teacher may wish to help students locate facts.

5. Once students have written three facts about their pets, they will draw a picture of them.

6. In science class, students may find more information about their animals through an animal CD-ROM, such as *ZOO-OPOLUS*.

## Learning Styles

Linguistic (reading and writing), intrapersonal (working alone), and spatial (drawing and imagining)

## Teaching Team

Library and science teachers

## Suggested Resources

Nonfiction books on pets and animals.

*ZOO-OPOLUS*. Novato, CA: The Learning Company, 1991 [CD-ROM].

# Catching the Rhythm

Write a rhyme for recess fun:

_____

_____

_____

_____

_____

## Standards

Students will

- Demonstrate a basic familiarity with selected fiction and poetry (McREL 11)
- Appreciate literature and other creative expressions (AASL/AECT 5)

## Objectives

Students recognize the rhythm of poetry by keeping a beat. Students repeat poems. Students copy a favorite poem.

## Directions

1. The library teacher locates some short catchy rhyming poems to share with the class. (An example of a good book for this lesson is *And the Green Grass Grew All Around: Folk Poetry for Everyone*. An easy-access poetry resource is the literature volume of the *Childcraft Encyclopedia*.) One example of a portion of a rhythmic poem for jumping rope or for keeping a beat would be

   > Cinderella dressed in yella,
   > Went downtown to meet her fella.

2. The library teacher copies two or three poems onto the board or an overhead transparency.
3. Students repeat the poems while keeping the beat by clapping, hopping, or snapping their fingers. The music teacher may help teach and have students use some rhythmic instruments to help keep the beat.
4. Students may also have some short rhyming poems of their own to share.
5. Students copy their favorite poem onto the rhythm worksheet.
6. The physical education teacher could have students repeat the rhymes as they jump rope or bounce a ball to the rhythm in the gym or outside.

## Learning Styles

Linguistic (reading), bodily kinesthetic (active), and musical (rhythm)

## Teaching Team

Library, music, and physical education teachers

## Suggested Resources

Books containing rhyming poems for children.

*Childcraft Encyclopedia: The How and Why Library.* Chicago: World Book, 2000.

Schwartz, Alvin. *And the Grass Grew All Around: Folk Poetry for Everyone.* New York: HarperCollins, 1992.

# The ABCs of Fiction

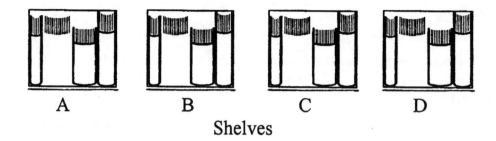

A        B        C        D

Shelves

Finding a fiction book is easy! Just look under the last name of the author. Look at this list of books. Circle the shelf where you would find the book.

Book                                          Which shelf is it on?

1. *The Gator Girls*
   by Stephanie Calmenson                      A   B   C   D

2. *Amber Brown Is Not a Crayon*
   by Paula Danziger                           A   B   C   D

3. *Franklin Fibs*
   by Paulette Bourgeois                       A   B   C   D

4. *Cupid Doesn't Flip Hamburgers*
   by Debbie Dadey                             A   B   C   D

5. *Madeline*
   by Ludwig Bemelman                          A   B   C   D

6. *Miss Nelson Is Missing*
   by Harry Allard                             A   B   C   D

7. *Berenstain Bears and the Spooky Old Tree*
   by Stan and Jan Berenstain                  A   B   C   D

## Standards

Students will

- Demonstrate a basic familiarity with selected fiction and poetry (McREL 11)
- Appreciate literature and other creative expressions (AASL/AECT 5)

## Objectives

Students learn how fiction books are organized in the library. Students locate favorite fiction book titles on worksheets. Students locate fiction books on the library shelves.

## Directions

1. The library teacher shows students that fiction books are arranged on the shelf by the first three letters of the author's last name. The teacher explains to students that they should start by looking on the shelf with the first letter of the author's last name. The teacher provides many examples of shelf locations for fiction books.

2. Student volunteers give examples of the shelf location of fiction books as guided by the teacher.

3. Students complete the fiction worksheet, where they locate a book title on the worksheet shelf by circling a letter.

4. If desired, students can look for some of the book titles on the worksheet, which includes second-graders' favorite books.

5. If there is time, the teacher may locate and read a brief fiction favorite.

6. In the language arts classroom, students may share more favorite fiction books.

## Learning Styles

Linguistic (reading and writing) and intrapersonal (working alone)

## Teaching Teams

Language arts and library teachers

## Suggested Resources

The fiction shelves of the library media center.

**My Space Adventure**

My Space Adventure

By _____

# Standards

Students will

- Comprehend the basic plot of simple stories (McREL 3)

- Share response to literature with peers (McREL 6)

- Demonstrate a basic familiarity with selected fiction and poetry (McREL 11)

- Appreciate literature and other creative expressions (AASL/AECT 5)

# Objectives

Students discuss plot after hearing a simple fantasy story. Students write their own fantasy story on worksheets.

# Directions

1. The library teacher reads an easy-reading fantasy book. (One example is *Spaceship Number Four* by Marjory Wunsch.)

2. Students discuss the plot. They discuss what parts make this book a fantasy.

3. Students think up their own fantasy adventure on the space adventure worksheet. Small groups or the whole class can work together on this project.

4. If desired, students could share their stories either in library or in language arts class. The language arts teacher may discuss which parts of each story make it a fantasy.

5. In art class, students may color and then glue their ships on flimsy paper plates. The space stories could be glued on the reverse side of the plates. The paper plate spaceships could be flown like Frisbees.

# Learning Styles

Linguistic (writing and telling stories), spatial (coloring), and intrapersonal (working alone)

# Teaching Team

Art, language arts, and library teachers

# Suggested Resources

Mazer, Anne. *Salamander Room*. New York: Alfred A. Knopf, 1994.

Wunsch, Marjory. *Spaceship Number Four: A Thanksgiving Story*. New York: Lothrop, Lee & Shepard Books, 1992.

# Chapter 4

## Third-Grade Lesson Plans

In order to create solid professional-based library lesson plans, the following selected Kendall and Marzano or McREL National Education Standards and Benchmarks for Kindergarten were chosen from the area of language arts, as it directly correlates with library information and appreciation skills. Furthermore, the AASL (American Association of School Libraries) and the AECT (Association for Educational Communications and Technology) list of Information Literacy Standards were applied to every lesson to ensure that all students will develop literary appreciation and will be effective users of information and ideas (listed in the Introduction). Teaching objectives were also given for each lesson as linked to the standards or active goals. Finally, Gardner's multiple intelligences are also integrated into each lesson, as all students have different methods of learning (also listed in the Introduction).

*Each lesson plan has a direct reference to the following numbered McREL benchmarks under the corresponding standards, as well as a direct reference to AASL/AECT standards.* Finally, all of the following twenty-minute lesson plans should be used in conjunction with the other teachers whenever possible. Moreover, all lesson plans are not the only means, but some of many, for library instruction. The following lessons can provide whole group discussion ideas, or they can provide individual or small group worksheet work.

# Third-Grade Library Standards and Then Bench-marks from Language Arts (McREL)*

Third-grade students will be able to

- Effectively gather and use information for research purposes (Standard 4)
    1. Use encyclopedias to gather information for research topics
    2. Use dictionaries to gather information for research topics
    3. Use key words, indexes, cross references, and letters on volumes to find information for research topics
    4. Use multiple representations of information (e.g., maps, charts) to find information for research topics
    5. Use the card catalog to locate books for research purposes (for grades 6–8)

- Demonstrate competence in general skills and strategies for reading literature (Standard 6)
    6. Become aware of the geographic location information important to the story one reads
    7. Share responses with peers
    8. Identify the main characters in works containing only a few basic characters
    9. Explain how characters or simple events in a work are like people or events in one's own life
    10. Recognize basic elements in plot

- Demonstrate competence in the general skills and strategies for reading information (Standard 7)
    11. Understand the uses of various book parts (index, table of contents, glossary, appendix)

- Demonstrate competence in applying the reading process to specific types of literary texts (Standard 8)
    12. Understand the defining features and structures of fantasies, fables, and fairy tales at this developmental level
    13. Understand the defining features and structures of myths and historical fiction
    14. Understand the defining features and structures of biographies and autobiographies

- Demonstrate a familiarity with selected literary works of enduring quality (Standard 13)
    15. Demonstrate a basic familiarity with a variety of classic fiction, folktales, and poetry
    16. Demonstrate a familiarity with a variety of selected nonfiction

## African Tales

 Read an African Story

Some examples of African stories include

*Anansi Goes Fishing*
*Anansi and the Moss-Covered Rock*
*Anansi the Spider: A Tale from Ashanti*
*A Story, A Story: An African Tale*
*Why Do Mosquitoes Buzz in People's Ears? A West African Story*
*The Village of Round and Square Houses*


Tell an African Story

- After reading an African story, pretend you are an African storyteller and tell the story to your classmates.
- You can make an African necklace or hat from the illustrations on this page.
- Practice telling the story. Make it sound exciting.
- Be sure and tell the story. Do not read it.

## Standards

Students will

- Share responses with peers (McREL 7)

- Demonstrate a basic familiarity with a variety of selected classic fiction, folktales, and poetry (McREL 15)

- Appreciate literature and other creative expressions (AASL/AECT 5)

- Recognize the importance of information to a democratic society (AASL/AECT 7)

## Objectives

Students listen to an African folktale. Students choose and learn an African folktale and practice being storytellers. Students make necklaces or storytelling hats.

## Directions

1. The library teacher explains that there are many folktales from different regions of Africa. African folktale suggestions are on the African Tales worksheet. This sheet can be copied onto an overhead transparency or onto copies for individual copies.

2. The class listens to an African folktale from the library teacher. The teacher may tell the story of *Anansi and the Moss-Covered Rock,* for example. Afterward, student pairs choose and read an African tale.

3. After choosing their folktale, students practice telling their African tales, first in library class and then in language arts class. Encourage the students to make storytelling fun. Tell them not to read their stories, but to tell them. They also may want to locate the African region from which their story originated so that they can tell this information as well.

4. In art class, the art teacher may help students make a paper necklace or a storytelling hat using the African-like symbols on the worksheet. For a hat, students can cut a sheet of construction paper in half vertically and then glue the ends together. Students glue their colored symbols on the hat. For a necklace, students can glue their symbols on yarn or roping. Students may then wear their hats or necklaces while telling their stories.

5. Finally, students tell their folktale stories to another grade level or to each other.

6. Students view the video of Anansi the Spider or play the *Anansi* CD-ROM.

## Learning Styles

Linguistic (reading and telling stories), interpersonal (working in groups), spatial (coloring), and intrapersonal (working alone)

## Teaching Team

Art, language arts, and library teachers

## Suggested Resources

*Anansi*. Toronto: Harmony Interactive, 1993 [CD-ROM].

*Anansi the Spider*. Chicago: Films Inc., 1989 [video].

Grifalconi, Ann. *The Village of Round and Square Houses*. Boston: Little, Brown, 1986.

Haley, Gail E. *A Story, A Story: An African Tale*. New York: Atheneum, 1988.

Kimmel, Eric. *Anansi and the Moss-Covered Rock*. New York: Scholastic, 1988.

Kimmel, Eric. *Anansi Goes Fishing*. New York: Holiday House, 1992.

McDermott, Gerald. *Anansi the Spider: A Tale from Ashanti*. New York: Econo-Clad Books, 1999.

# John Henry

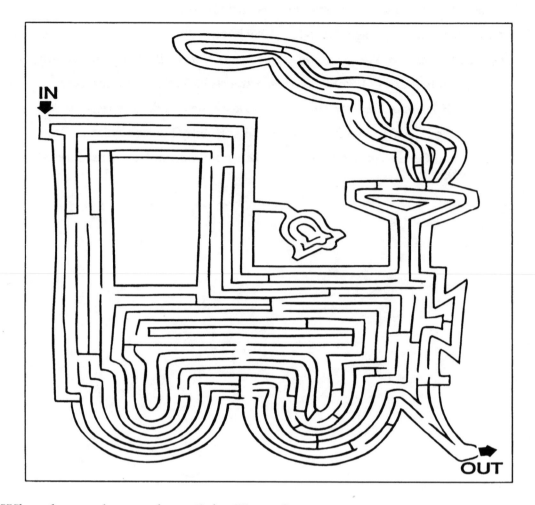

1. What do you know about John Henry? _____

_____

2. What is the story's plot? _____

_____

3. What parts of the story really happened? _____

_____

4. John Henry worked on the railroad. Can you work your way through the train maze?

## Standards

Students will

- Identify the main characters in works containing only a few basic characters (McREL 8)
- Recognize basic elements in plot (McREL 10)
- Demonstrate a basic familiarity with a variety of classic fiction, folktales, and poetry (McREL 15)
- Appreciate literature and other creative expressions (AASL/AECT 5)
- Participate effectively in groups to pursue and generate information (AASL/AECT 9)

## Objectives

After listening to the legend of John Henry, students will discuss and write down the plot and story parts. Students discuss what made John Henry a legend. Students complete the train maze.

## Directions

1. The teacher tells the legend of John Henry to the class. The teacher will need to locate an easy-reading version of *John Henry*. An example is the Caldecott Medal winner illustrated by Jerry Pinkney and written by Julius Lester.

2. There are many good videos and audiotapes about John Henry. Perhaps one of these could be used in the place of the book. (Weston Woods has produced a video of Lester's version of *John Henry*.)

3. After hearing or viewing *John Henry*, the class discusses what made John Henry a legend. Answers might include his strength, the fact that he never gave up, and his desire to work hard. Students will write their answers on the John Henry worksheets as guided by the teacher and through class discussion.

4. The class discusses and answers the rest of the worksheet questions as a whole group.

5. Then students can do the train maze.

6. If there is time, students draw a picture of John Henry in the train window.

7. This lesson provides a good introductory lesson on legends for the language arts classroom. The language arts teacher may want to read and discuss another legend, such as the elementary version of the *Legend of Sleepy Hollow* by Will Moses.

## Learning Styles

Linguistic (writing), spatial (puzzles), mathematical (thinking logically), and interpersonal (working in groups)

## Teaching Team

Language arts and library teachers

## Suggested Resources

Any version of the John Henry tale.

*John Henry.* Westport, CT: Weston Woods, 1998 [video].

Keats, Ezra Jack. *John Henry: An American Legend.* New York: Scholastic, 1965.

Lester, Julius. Jerry Pinkney, illustrator. *John Henry.* New York: Dial Books for Young Readers, 1994.

Moses, Will. *Legend of Sleepy Hollow.* New York: Putnam Books for Young Readers, 1995.

# Our 3rd Grade Autobiography

---

I am _____
                    (Name)

I was born on _____

I am going to school at _____

I am famous for _____

_____

Some day, I will be _____

Draw a picture of yourself:

## Standards

Students will

- Share responses with peers (McREL 7)
- Understand the defining features and structures of biographies and autobiographies (McREL 14)
- Pursue information related to personal interest (AASL/AECT 4)
- Appreciate literature and other creative expressions (AASL/AECT 5)
- Recognize the importance of information to a democratic society (AASL/AECT 7)

## Objectives

Students will understand what makes up biographies and autobiographies. Students write and illustrate brief autobiographies that will be collected into a class booklet.

## Directions

1. The library teacher explains that biographies are true stories about famous people such as presidents, inventors, scientists, explorers, athletes, and others. Students think of examples of people who may have books written about them. The library teacher should show students some examples of biographies and autobiographies.

2. The library teacher explains that autobiographies are biographies written by the subject of the book. The language arts teacher may want to team teach this lesson.

3. Students will make a collective class autobiography. Each student makes a brief autobiography while using the bottom sheet from the autobiography worksheet. The top of the worksheet has the title sheet for the class autobiography booklet.

4. Students write when they were born, where they go to school, why they are famous, and what their future goals are. (Students may proclaim that they are not famous at all. However, the teacher can point out that students are famous for their sports, friendliness, creativity, spelling, nice smiles, and so on.)

5. In language arts class, students may type their autobiography sheets on a word-processing program such as the Student Writing Center. Students will illustrate their pages after they are done typing.

6. Student pages are stapled together for the collective autobiography booklet. The booklet's cover, "Our Third-Grade Autobiographies," will be attached to the finished product. The booklet can be displayed in the classroom.

## Learning Styles

Linguistic (reading and writing), intrapersonal (working alone), and spatial (drawing)

## Teaching Team

Language arts and library teachers

## Suggested Resources

The biography section of the library media center.

*Student Writing Center.* Novato, CA: The Learning Company, 2000 [computer program].

# Searching for Books

Start Searching! Search the card catalog.
1. Pick a subject.
2. Choose a book.
3. Write the book title down.
4. Find the book!

## Subject Search 1

What is the *subject* (what are you trying to find)? _____

What is the *title* of the book? _____

What is the book's *call number*? _____
                                    _____

## Subject Search 2

What is the *subject* (what are you trying to find)? _____

What is the *title* of the book? _____

What is the book's *call number*? _____
                                    _____

## Standards

Students will

- Use the card catalog to locate books for research purposes (McREL 5)
- Access information efficiently and effectively (AASL/AECT 1)
- Pursue information related to personal interest (AASL/AECT 4)
- Strive for excellence in information seeking (AASL/AECT 6)
- Practice ethical behavior in regard to information and information technology (AASL/AECT 8)

## Objectives

Students learn to locate books with the automated and paper card catalogs. Students choose a subject and then search the card catalog to find two books on their subject. Students write down the subjects, titles, and call numbers on their worksheets. Students locate their books in the library.

## Directions

1. Students need to know how to use the automated card catalog. The library teacher may wish to use a computer connected to a display medium (such as an LCD projector) to show students how to use the card catalog. If a projector is not available, students may gather in small groups around different card catalog computer stations for instruction. If the library is not automated, the library teacher should make an overhead transparency of the three main card catalog cards.

2. The teacher shows students how to do subject, title, and author searching with the card catalog.

3. The teacher shows students where the call number is located with either the use of the computerized card catalog screen or with the overhead projector. The teacher reminds students where to locate the title and author on the catalog cards.

4. Small student groups begin using the card catalog. Small groups of students search card catalog stations for books on their chosen subjects. To save time, the library teacher may assign topics.

5. Once two books are found on the card catalog, students will write down the pertinent information needed to find the books (book title, call number, and the subject searched).

6. Students will find the books located with their card catalog search.

7. For reinforced learning, the language arts class could visit the library to locate certain topics on the card catalog.

## Learning Styles

Linguistic (reading), mathematical (computers), interpersonal (group work), bodily kinesthetic (moving around)

## Teaching Team

Language arts and library teachers

## Suggested Resources

An LCD or Proxima projector and the card catalog computer stations.

# Diving into Dictionaries

Write down some reasons why someone might use a dictionary.

1. _____

2. _____

3. _____

Now use a dictionary. Find the meanings of the following words:

**1. Computer** _____

_____

_____

**2. Research** _____

_____

_____

**3. Library** _____

_____

_____

**4. Catalog** _____

_____

_____

## Standards

Students will

- Use dictionaries to gather information for research topics (McREL 2)
- Access information efficiently and effectively (AASL/AECT 1)
- Evaluate information critically and competently (AASL/AECT 2)
- Use information accurately and creatively (AASL/AECT 3)
- Strive for excellence in information seeking (AASL/AECT 6)
- Participate effectively in groups to pursue and generate information (AASL/AECT 9)

## Objectives

Students discuss the uses of dictionaries. Groups of students search dictionaries for definitions of words found on their worksheets.

## Directions

1.  The library teacher asks the class to discuss the uses of dictionaries (for instance, dictionaries are used to find word meaning, pronunciation, spelling, word origin, and so on).
2.  The library teacher points out the library reference shelf location of dictionaries.
3.  The teacher provides multiple copies of dictionaries. Students are grouped according to the number of available dictionaries.
4.  Students answer the questions on the dictionary worksheet.
5.  If there is time, students find a word associated with a teacher-selected topic, such as computers (software, monitor, microchip, printer, keyboard, disk, memory, and so on). Students write down the words and then the meanings on the back of their worksheets.
6.  This dictionary lesson provides an introduction or review of dictionaries for the main classroom. The language arts teachers could have students locate more words in their classroom. For instance, students could use dictionaries to look up the week's spelling words.

## Learning Styles

Linguistic (reading and writing), mathematical (thinking logically), and interpersonal (group work)

## Teaching Team

Language arts and library teachers

## Suggested Resources

Multiple dictionaries.

# Hopping into Spring

## Standards

Students will

- Demonstrate a basic familiarity with a variety of classic fiction, folktales, and poetry (McREL 15)

- Demonstrate a familiarity with a variety of selected nonfiction (McREL 16)

- Access information efficiently and effectively (AASL/AECT 1)

- Evaluate information critically and competently (AASL/AECT 2)

- Use information accurately and creatively (AASL/AECT 3)

## Objectives

Groups of students locate information about rabbits. Students list single-word rabbit facts to create altered cinquain poems about rabbits. Students write their poems on worksheets or on rabbit greeting cards.

## Directions

1.  The library teacher copies the rabbit worksheets onto springtime-colored paper. (Students can create greeting cards if the sheets are copied onto stiffer paper.)

2.  Groups of students or the class as a whole write an altered cinquain poem about rabbits after discovering some rabbit facts. An altered cinquain poem follows this pattern:

    | First line | = | a one word title |
    |---|---|---|
    | Second line | = | two words to describe the title |
    | Third line | = | three words to express an action |
    | Fourth line | = | four words to express a feeling |
    | Fifth line | = | one or two words to restate the title |

3.  Give students a few minutes to locate some brief rabbit facts using nonfiction sources, such as *Rabbit* by Mark Evan or *Rabbits, Rabbits, and More Rabbits* by Gail Gibbons, or the encyclopedia.

4.  After listing single-word rabbit facts, small groups or the class creates an altered cinquain poem such as

    Rabbits

    Fluffy, Fast

    Hopping, Hiding, Running

    Nice, Fun, Lovable, Cute

    Easter Bunnies

5.  Students will copy their poems on the rabbit worksheets. The students may color the worksheets.

6.  In art class, the poems may be made into greeting cards by stapling the poem to the rabbit. Poems may also be typed using a computer program such as *Print Shop Deluxe* to make computer-generated cards.

## Learning Styles

Linguistic (reading and writing), interpersonal (working together), spatial (coloring), and musical (rhythm of poetry)

## Teaching Team

Art and library teachers

## Suggested Resources

Evan, Mark. *Rabbit*. New York: Dorling Kindersley, 1992.

Gibbons, Gail. *Rabbits, Rabbits, and More Rabbits*. New York: Holiday House, 2000.

*Print Shop Deluxe*. Novato, CA: The Learning Company, 2000 [CD-ROM].

# The Fable of the Fox and the Grapes

Once upon a time, a fox was wandering around. He came upon two birds eating grapes from the vines that grew on the wall. The fox tried to reach the grapes, but he could not. He kept jumping and jumping, but he just could not reach those grapes.

As the birds ate the grapes, they kept saying how delicious they were. This made the fox even hungrier for the grapes. So he kept on jumping for them. He still couldn't reach them.

Finally, the hungry fox gave up. He told the birds, "Those grapes are probably sour anyway. I really don't want them, so there!"

The birds said, "You would not be calling them sour grapes if you were the one who could reach them."

**Discussion**

1. A fable is a story with animal characters who talk and act like people. Who were the main characters is this fable?

2. The most important things about fables are that they teach a lesson or a moral. What is the moral or lesson of this fable?

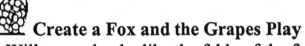 **Create a Fox and the Grapes Play**

1. Will your play be like the fable of the fox and the grapes? Will it be different?

2. Who will be the actors?  What will the actors say?

# Standards

Students will

- Identify the main characters in works containing only a few basic characters (McREL 8)

- Explain how characters or simple events in a work are like people or events in one's own life (McREL 9)

- Understand the defining features and structures of fantasies, fables, and fairy tales at this developmental level (McREL 12)

- Appreciate literature and other creative expressions (AASL/AECT 5)

- Recognize the importance of information to a democratic society (AASL/AECT 7)

# Objectives

Students discuss plot, characters, and the moral of *The Fable of the Fox and the Grapes* after hearing it. Students will write a simple play using the same characters and similar moral, but with a slightly different setting. Students perform their plays.

# Directions

1. The teacher makes a transparency of The Fable of the Fox and the Grapes worksheet so that the class can refer to it for later work.

2. The library teacher introduces fables by saying that fables have animals that act and talk like people. Fables have a moral or lesson to be learned.

3. The library teacher reads the fable from the transparency.

4. After hearing and discussing the fable, students will work in small groups to create a play of the fable. Students should be encouraged to slightly modify the original fable version, as long as the moral and characters stay the same.

5. The script should be simple. Once groups settle on their story, they will decide who will play the fox and who will play the birds. Students then decide what the actors or performers will say. (Students will need about five to ten minutes to create a brief oral script.)

6. In art class, student groups may create simple backgrounds for their plays.

7. In language arts class, students may wish to practice and then perform their plays.

8. As a follow-up, students can see the video titled *Three Fox Fables*.

# Learning Styles

Linguistic (reading and writing), spatial (creating visually), and bodily kinesthetic (acting)

# Teaching Team

Art, language art, and library teachers

# Suggested Resources

*Three Fox Fables.* Chicago: (EB) Encyclopedia Britannica Producers, 1984 [video].

# Cinderella

Read Cinderella. Now read another version of Cinderella. Compare them. Did both of them have a castle ending?

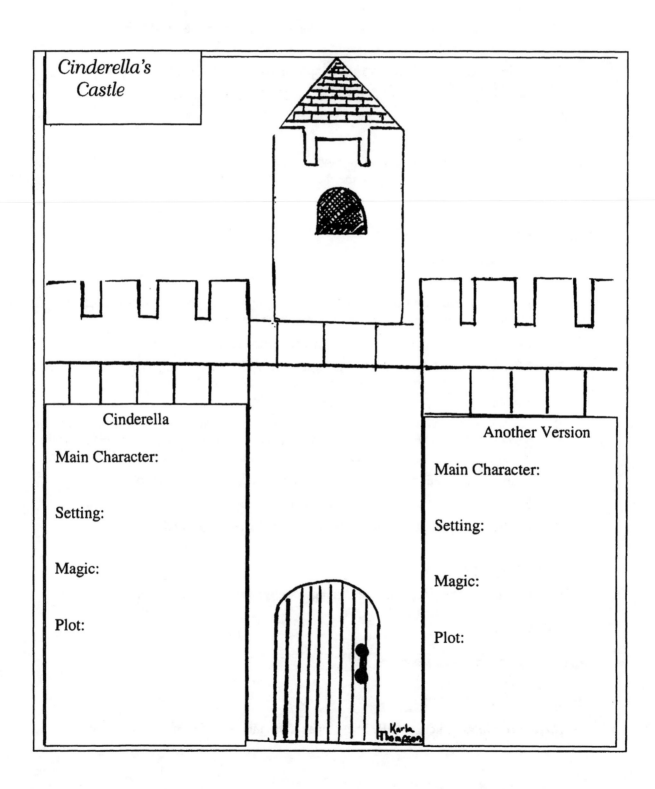

*Cinderella's Castle*

Cinderella

Main Character:

Setting:

Magic:

Plot:

Another Version

Main Character:

Setting:

Magic:

Plot:

# Standards

Students will

- Become aware of the geographic location important to the story one reads (McREL 6)
- Share responses with peers (McREL 7)
- Identify the main characters in works containing only a few basic characters (McREL 8)
- Recognize basic elements of plot (McREL 10)
- Understand the defining features and structures and structures of fantasies, fables, and fairy tales at this developmental level (McREL 12)
- Appreciate literature and other creative expressions (AASL/AECT 5)

# Objectives

Students discuss and write down the main character, the setting, and the plot from two Cinderella stories. Students compare stories.

# Directions

1. Students compare two different versions of *Cinderella*. (Two of the many versions are the retold Marcia Brown's French version, Caldecott Medal book winner *Cinderella* and the Vietnamese version called *Tam's Slipper: A Story from Vietnam*.)

2. Students compare two versions of *Cinderella* on the castle worksheet after hearing them. The class will discuss the main character, the setting, the magic that occurred, and the main plot from each version.

3. Students discuss how the stories were the same and how they were different.

4. In the main classroom, the language arts teacher may have the class listen and compare another version of Cinderella, titled *Sootface: An Ojibwa Cinderella* by Robert San Souci, *Raisel's Riddle* by Erica Silverman, or *The Korean Cinderella* by Shirley Climo.

5. Library or language arts students may also watch the *Cinderella* CD-ROM.

# Learning Styles

Linguistic (writing), interpersonal (group work), and intrapersonal (working alone)

# Teaching Team

Language arts and library teachers

# Suggested Resources

Brown, Marcia. *Cinderella*. New York: Atheneum, 1971.

*Cinderella*. Phoenix, AZ: BFA, 1981 [video].

*Cinderella*. Toronto, Canada: Harmony Interactive, 1990 [CD-ROM].

Climo, Shirley. *The Korean Cinderella*. New York: HarperCollins, 1993.

Palazzo-Craig. *Tam's Slipper: A Story from Vietnam*. Mahwah, NJ: Troll, 1996.

San Souci, Robert. *Sootface: An Ojibwa Cinderella*. New York: Delacorte Press, 1994.

Silverman, Erica. *Raisel's Riddle*. New York: Farrar, Straus & Giroux, 1999.

# Peter Pan Adventures

   All stories have three parts: a beginning, middle, and an ending.  Illustrate the three parts of *Peter Pan*.

1.  Illustrate the beginning of *Peter Pan*.

2.  Illustrate the middle of *Peter Pan*.

3.  Illustrate the ending of *Peter Pan*.

# Standards

Students will

- Understand the defining features and structures of fantasies, fables, and fairy tales at this developmental level (McREL 12)

- Demonstrate a basic familiarity with a variety of selected classic fiction, folktales, and poetry (McREL 15)

- Appreciate literature and other creative expressions (AASL/AECT 5)

# Objectives

Students discuss the parts of a story that makes it a fantasy story. Students illustrate three main parts of the fantasy story of *Peter Pan* as they hear it.

# Directions

1. The library teacher makes copies of the Peter Pan worksheet. The teacher reads an easy-reading version of *Peter Pan* to the class. (One example is *Peter Pan* by Monique Peterson.)

2. The library teacher introduces the story of *Peter Pan* by explaining that it is a fantasy. That is, it includes things that sound like it could happen in the real world but then changes as the story unveils itself. As the teacher is reading the story, he or she may stop and point out the parts that are fantasy or ask the students to do so.

3. Students illustrate the three main parts of the story on the worksheet. After the teacher has read the first part, the class will be directed to start illustrating that part. The teacher will then repeat this method of reading and stopping for student illustrating for each subsequent part.

4. After the worksheets are completed, class discussion should continue about the fantasy parts of *Peter Pan.*

5. Provide time for students to share their illustrations.

6. The language arts teacher may continue the discussion of fantasy books in the main classroom. Perhaps the class may look at another easy-reading book version of a fantasy story such as *Alice in Wonderland*, retold by Jane Fior.

# Learning Styles

Spatial (drawing), interpersonal (group discussion), and intrapersonal (working alone)

# Teaching Team

Language arts and library teachers

# Suggested Resources

An easy-reading version of the Peter Pan story.

Fior, Jane, retold. *Alice in Wonderland.* New York: Dorling Kindersley, 2000.

Shebar, James, retold. *Peter Pan.* Mahwah, NJ: Troll, 1988.

# Your Island Adventure

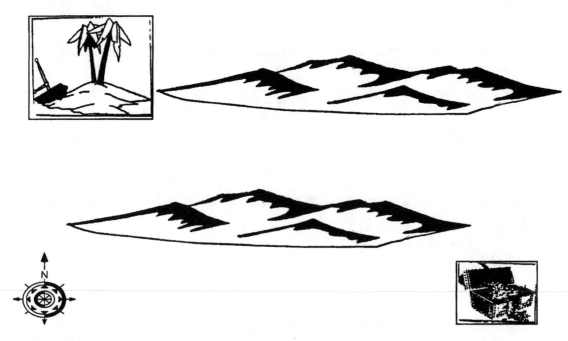

Your boat has crashed on an island. Your treasure chest has floated to the other side of the island. How will you get your treasure? Finish the map.

1. First you will need directions, so you won't get lost. Label your compass: Look for the letter N for north. Now write the letters S for south, W for west, and E for east.

2. How will you survive? On the map, draw a river that flows south between the mountains. Then you will have water to drink. Now, move on.

3. You'll need to build a boat to get back your treasure. For wood to make a boat, draw some trees near the east side of one of the mountains.

4. Now how will you get to your treasure box? Which direction will you go with your boat? Circle the right direction: north, south, west, or east.

5. What happened? Write a paragraph to describe your island adventure.

## Standards

Students will

- Use multiple representations of information (e.g., maps, charts) to find information for research topics (McREL 4)
- Access information efficiently and effectively (AASL/AECT 1)
- Evaluate information critically and competently (AASL/AECT 2)
- Use information accurately and creatively (AASL/AECT 3)

## Objectives

Students will use map skills to locate places directed on the island worksheets. Students write a paragraph on imaginary island adventures.

## Directions

1.  This lesson centers on an imaginative story in which students will need to use their map skills. The library teacher will provide copies of the worksheet.

2.  The library teacher points out the compass rose on the map. The students note the N on the compass rose to direct them for future use on the worksheet.

3.  After reading the beginning paragraph, pairs of students or individuals complete their worksheet adventure. They finish filling in the map according to worksheet directions. As they fill in the map, students will come closer to getting their treasures back.

4.  After completing their worksheet map, students write a brief paragraph on their island adventure in library class or in language arts class. The paragraph can be written on the back of the worksheet or on separate page. Students may want to write about falling into quick sand, meeting a crocodile, swinging by vines like Tarzan, meeting hungry wild pigs, discovering pirates, being trapped from traveling by beautiful island waterfalls, meeting curious monkeys, and so on.

5.  Students may wish to share their island stories.

6.  If time permits, students may browse through atlases to become familiar with other types of maps.

7.  This lesson provides either a good introduction or a review of map skills for the social studies teacher. Moreover, the social studies teacher could have students locate places on actual maps.

## Learning Styles

Spatial (maps and thinking visually), mathematical (thinking logically), intrapersonal (working alone), and linguistic (writing and reading)

## Teaching Team

Language arts, library, and social studies teachers

## Suggested Resources

Atlases.

# Farmer Boy

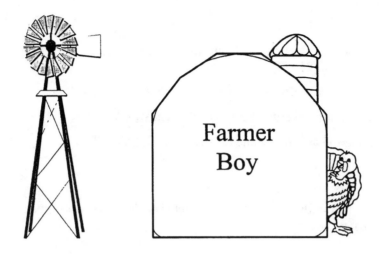

1. Who is the main character of *Farmer Boy?* _____

2. List some of the supporting characters. _____

_____

_____

_____

3. Where is the geographic location (or the setting) of the story?

_____

4. What is the story's plot? _____

_____

_____

_____

_____

5. On a separate sheet, illustrate part of the story that could only happen back in olden times.

# Standards

Students will

- Become aware of the geographic information important to the story one reads (McREL 6)

- Share responses with peers (McREL 7)

- Identify the main characters in works containing only a few basic characters (McREL 8)

- Explain how characters or simple events in a work are like people or events in one's own life (McREL 9)

- Understand defining features and structures of myths and historical fiction (McREL 13)

- Appreciate literature and other creative expressions (AASL/AECT 5)

# Objectives

Students discuss and write down the main plot, characters, and setting while hearing the chapter book version of *Farmer Boy*. Students will illustrate a historical part of the book.

# Directions

1. The library teacher will read to the class the chapter book version of *Farmer Boy* by Laura Ingalls Wilder. This version will not take as much time, compared to the original version. Read the book a section at a time, while stopping for discussion when the situation merits.

2. Remind students what makes up a story's main plot, its main character, its supporting characters, and its setting. During class discussion, students will answer questions concerning plot, character, and so on using their farm worksheets.

3. The language arts teacher could have the class complete the story and the discussion within the main classroom.

4. The social studies teacher or the library teacher could have the class illustrate a part of the story that illuminates that period in history.

# Learning Styles

Linguistic (writing), interpersonal (working together), and mathematical (thinking logically)

# Teaching Team

Language arts, library, and social studies teachers

# Suggested Resources

Wilder, Laura Ingalls. *Farmer Boy Days*. New York: HarperCollins, 1998.

## Searching for Key Words

Key words help you find things in the encyclopedia.
**Directions:** (1) Circle the key words in these questions. (2) Then find the answers.

1. How big is a deer?  Answer: _____

2. How many rooms are in the White House?  Answer: _____

3. Why was Benjamin Franklin famous?  Answer: _____

4. Where do alligators live?  Answer: _____

5. Where are the Rocky Mountains?  Answer: _____

6. How is paper made?  Answer briefly: _____

_____

_____

**Did you find answers
with your key words?
Good going!**

# Standards

Students will

- Use encyclopedias to gather information for research topics (McREL 1)
- Use key word, indexes, cross references, and letters on volumes to find information for research topics (McREL 3)
- Access information efficiently and effectively (AASL/AECT 1)
- Evaluate information critically and competently (AASL/AECT 2)
- Use information accurately and creatively (AASL/AECT 3)
- Strive for excellence in information seeking (AASL/AECT 6)
- Practice ethical behavior in regard to information and information technology (AASL/AECT 8)
- Participate effectively in groups to pursue and generate information (AASL/AECT 9)

# Objectives

Student groups locate key words in encyclopedias. Students will use encyclopedias to find the answers to the worksheet questions.

# Directions

1. The library teacher reminds students that key words help people find information much more quickly. The teacher also reminds students that a person in the encyclopedia is located under their last name.

2. The teacher provides students with the key word worksheets, unless an overhead transparency is created. Also, the class needs access to encyclopedias. Instruct students to look at the encyclopedia captions before attempting to skim the entire article.

3. The class will do one worksheet question as a group to introduce this activity. Students first guess which word in the question is the key word and then circle it. Then the class looks the word up in the encyclopedia to see if they were correct.

4. Next small groups of students complete the worksheets. They will circle a possible key word for each worksheet question, and then look it up to see if they were correct. When they find a correct answer, students will write it on the worksheet.

5. If there is time, the students can compare their answers.

6. In language arts or social studies class, students can locate key words in textbooks to reinforce the location of key words.

# Learning Styles

Linguistic (reading and writing), interpersonal (working together), and bodily kinesthetic (moving around)

# Teaching Team

Language arts, library, and science teachers

# Suggested Resources

Any encyclopedia sets suitable for this grade level or the *World Book Encyclopedia*.

# Solving the Mysteries of Title Pages

*The Mystery at Lime Creek*

By Jan Keeling
Illustrated by Chad Keeling

Gold Press       New York

**Look at *The Mystery at Lime Creek* title page to answer these questions:**

1. What is the title of this book? _____

2. Who is the author? _____

3. Who is the illustrator? _____

4. Who is the publisher that printed the book? _____

5. Where was the book published? _____

Now find a title page from an actual book to answer these questions:

1. What is the title? _____

2. Who is the author? _____

3. Who is the illustrator? _____

4. Who is the publisher? _____

5. Where was it published? _____

6. Is there a picture or illustration on your title page? Draw it on the back of this sheet.

# Standards

Students will

- Understand the various book parts (index, table of contents, glossary, appendix) (McREL 11)
- Access information efficiently and effectively (AASL/AECT 1)
- Strive for excellence in information seeking (AASL/AECT 6)

# Objectives

Students define parts of the title page (author, title, illustrator, publisher, and place of publication) for a worksheet sample and then for an actual book.

# Directions

1. The library teacher provides students with worksheets and then shows and defines the various parts of the title page with a book. The title page parts include the title, author, illustrator, publisher, and place of publication.

2. Students will find the title page parts according to the example found on their worksheets. This example could be developed into an overhead transparency for the class to complete as a group.

3. Then student pairs will find an actual book and use it to identify the title page parts. They will write that information on the bottom half of their worksheets.

4. If time permits, partners will find other books and identify the title page parts with each other. The library teacher checks for understanding as the partners work together.

5. As a review, the language arts teacher may have students identify the title page parts of textbooks or other books in English class.

# Learning Styles

Linguistic (writing), bodily kinesthetic (moving around), and interpersonal (working in pairs)

# Teaching Teams

Language arts and library teachers

# Suggested Resources

Any books.

## Celebrating Hanukkah!

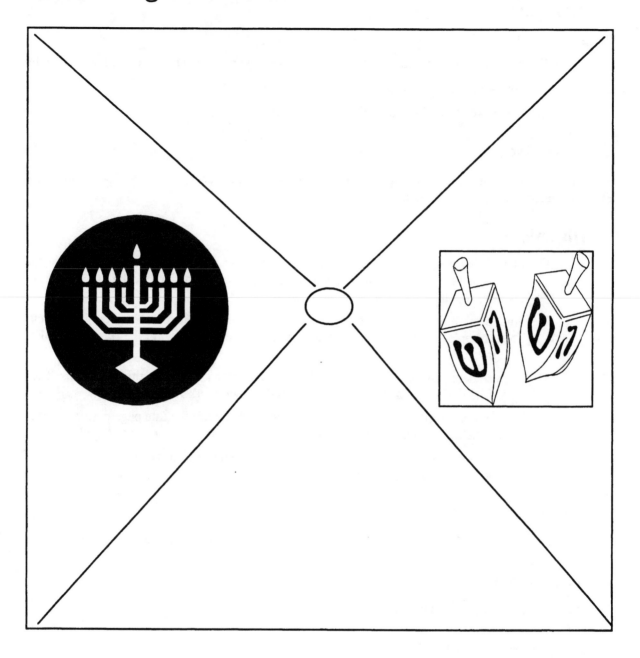

*Draw two more things that have to do with Hanukkah.*
*Now, decorate your pinwheel!*

## Standards

Students will

- Explain how characters or simple events in a work are like people or events in one's own life (McREL 9)

- Recognize basic elements of plot (McREL 10)

- Use information accurately and creatively (AASL/AECT 3)

- Recognize the importance of information to a democratic society (AASL/AECT 7)

- Practice ethical behavior in regard to information and information technology (AACL/AECT 8)

## Objectives

Students list symbolic Hanukkah objects after hearing fiction and nonfiction books. Students create a Hanukkah pinwheel featuring the symbols.

## Directions

1. Students learn about Hanukkah through one or two easy-reading fiction books (such as *Inside-Out Grandma: A Hanukkah Story* by Joan Rohenberg, *Borrowed Hanukkah Latkes* by Linda Glaser, or *All the Lights in the Night* by Arthur Levine). Students also learn about Hanukkah from nonfiction sources (such as *Celebrations Around the World: A Multicultural Handbook* by Carole Angell or *Celebrations of Light: A Year of Holidays Around the World* by Nancy Luenn).

2. The library teacher first reads about Hanukkah from a nonfiction source. Then the teacher reads one or two Hanukkah fiction books.

3. On the board, students will list different symbolic objects associated with Hanukkah as learned from the resources. List these objects on the board.

4. The art or library teacher asks students to make a Hanukkah pinwheel from the worksheet. Two objects representing Hanukkah are already drawn on pinwheel slots. Students draw two other objects that represent Hanukkah as learned from Hanukkah stories or nonfiction sources. Students should be reminded not to trace objects from their sources, but to create their own drawings.

5. After drawing and coloring their pinwheels, students fold on the inside lines.

6. Pinwheels may be taped to the top of straws or pinned to the top of student pencils.

## Learning Styles

Spatial (drawing and coloring), intrapersonal (working alone), and bodily kinesthetic (crafts)

## Teaching Team

Art and library teachers

## Suggested Resources

Angell, Carole. *Celebrations Around the World: A Multicultural Handbook*. New York: Fulcrum, 1996.

Glaser, Linda. *Borrowed Hanukkah Latkes*. Morton Grove, IL: Whitman, 1997.

Levine, Arthur. *All the Lights in the Night*. New York: Tambourine Books, 1991.

Luenn, Nancy. *Celebrations of Light: A Year of Holidays Around the World*. New York: Atheneum, 1998.

Rohenberg, Joan. *Inside-Out Grandma: A Hanukkah Story*. New York: Hyperion, 1995.

# Encyclopedia Searching

**1. The ABC (alphabetical) order of encyclopedia volumes helps you find information. Find the volume and page number for these key words:**

| Key Word | Volume | Page |
|---|---|---|
| Shark | v. | p. |
| Iguanas | v. | p. |
| Olympics | v. | p. |
| Ben Franklin | v. | p. |
| Tornado | v. | p. |

**2. Encyclopedia volumes have one big index. Look at the index to find the volumes and page numbers for these key words:**

| Key Word | Volume | Page |
|---|---|---|
| Giant Octopus | v. | p. |
| Indian Tribes | v. | p. |

# Standards

Students will

- Use encyclopedias to gather information for research purposes (McREL 1)
- Use key words, indexes, cross references, and letters on volumes to find information for research topics (McREL 3)
- Share responses with peers (McREL 7)
- Access information efficiently and effectively (AASL/AECT 1)
- Evaluate information critically and competently (AASL/AECT 2)
- Use information accurately and creatively (AASL/AECT 3)
- Practice ethical behavior in regard to information and information technology (AASL/AECT 8)

# Objectives

Students review encyclopedia skills. Small student groups locate and write volume and page numbers for key words in print encyclopedias on worksheets. Small student groups locate key words in print encyclopedia indexes for the worksheets. Students locate key words using electronic encyclopedias.

# Directions

1. The library teacher makes sure that there is more than one encyclopedia set available, unless successful sharing can be accomplished with one set. The *World Book Encyclopedia* could be used for this lesson because this is an easier set for this age level.

2. The teacher provides students with copies of the encyclopedia worksheet.

3. The library teacher shows and reminds students that the entire encyclopedia set has a single index in one volume.

4. The teacher reads the worksheet directions to the students and tells them to look first at the volumes and then at the index.

5. Students work in small groups to complete the worksheets.

6. After completing their worksheet searches, students may look up one of the key words to find one or two interesting facts. Students may then share those facts with the class.

7. As a follow-up, the language arts or the library teacher may have students use a CD-ROM encyclopedia (such as *Microsoft Encarta Multimedia*).

# Learning Styles

Linguistic (reading, writing, trivia), mathematical (challenging activities), interpersonal (working together), and bodily kinesthetic (moving around)

# Teaching Team

Language arts and library teachers

# Suggested Resources

Any encyclopedias, such as the *World Book Encyclopedia*.

*Microsoft Encarta Encyclopedia Deluxe 2001*. Richmond, WA: Microsoft, 2001 [CD-ROM].

# Valentines

## Standards

Students will

- Demonstrate a basic familiarity with a variety of classic fiction, folktales, and poetry (McREL 15)
- Demonstrate a familiarity with a variety of selected nonfiction (McREL 16)
- Access information efficiently and effectively (AASL/AECT 1)
- Use information accurately and creatively (AASL/AECT 3)
- Pursue information related to personal interest (AASL/AECT 4)
- Appreciate literature and other creative expressions (AASL/AECT 5)

## Objectives

Students find a brief poem for Valentine's Day. Students write their poems on the worksheet valentine. Students may either create valentine cards or valentine puzzles with the worksheets.

## Directions

1. The library teacher may want to copy the valentine worksheets in pink and red colors. If the students are going to make puzzles, the worksheets should be copied onto sturdier paper.

2. The library teacher gives some examples of poems and poetry books for Valentine's Day. (The teacher may find examples in sources such as Myra Cohn Livingston's *I Like You, If You Like Me: Poems of Friendship* and *It's Valentine's Day* by Jack Prelutsky.)

3. Direct students toward the poetry section of the library to find a short poem.

4. Students write their poems on the valentine heart worksheets.

5. Students will either decorate their valentine sheets as greeting cards or they can create valentine puzzles. This portion of the lesson can be completed in art or library class.

6. If students wish to have their worksheet hearts become a Valentine's Day puzzle, they can cut the hearts into six or more pieces.

## Learning Styles

Linguistic (reading and writing), intrapersonal (working alone), spatial (puzzles), and musical (rhythm of poetry)

## Teaching Team

Art and library teachers

## Suggested Resources

Livingston, Myra Cohn. *I Like You, If You Like Me: Poems of Friendship*. New York: McElderry Books, 1987.

Prelutsky, Jack. *It's Valentine's Day*. New York: Greenwillow Books, 1983.

# African Safari

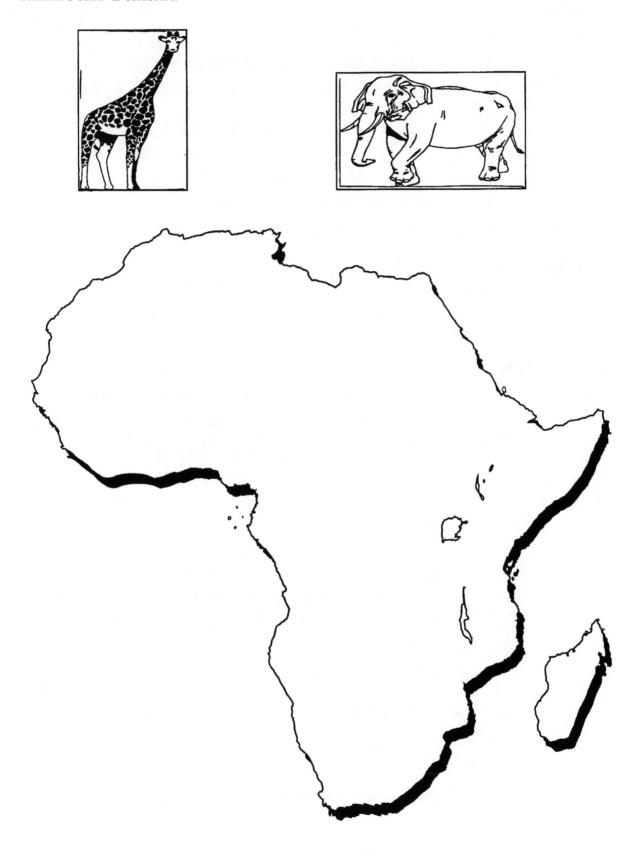

## Standards

Students will

- Use encyclopedias to gather information for research purposes (McREL 1)
- Use multiple representations of information (e.g., maps, charts) to find information for research topics (McREL 4)
- Use the card catalog to locate books for research purposes (McREL5)
- Demonstrate a familiarity with a variety of selection nonfiction (McREL16)
- Access information efficiently and effectively (AASL/AECT 1)
- Pursue information related to personal interest (AASL/AECT 4)
- Recognize the importance of information to a democratic society (AASL/AECT 7)

## Objectives

Students find information about a chosen African animal. Students write one paragraph about their animal. Students draw or copy a picture of their animal. Students find the locality of their animal so that they can mark its dwelling place(s) on the worksheet map.

## Directions

1. Students will go on an African safari by means of researching African animals.
2. The library teacher will ask students to select an African animal from a suggested list. (In order to create the suggested list, the teacher can find a map showing African animals and their locations under "Africa" in the *World Book Encyclopedia*.)
3. Students choose an African animal and then use the card catalog to find a nonfiction book.
4. Students use nonfiction books to write one factual paragraph about their animal. Paragraphs should be about four sentences long. The science teacher may want to assist in this project.
5. Students could draw a small picture of their animal, or they could copy their animal's picture from the Internet. This portion of the project may be done in art class.
6. Students will find out where their animals are located on the African continent. (For example, they may look up "Africa" in the *World Book Encyclopedia* to find the location map of African animals.) Then they will use their African map worksheets to mark their animals' location by attaching their animal picture to that spot.
7. Students may also place their paragraphs on the African map sheets and then display them.
8. The social studies teacher may have students do additional research, focusing on African countries.

## Learning Styles

Linguistic (reading and writing) and spatial (creating)

## Teaching Team

Art, library, science, and social studies teachers

## Suggested Resources

Nonfiction animal sources or encyclopedias.

## Pandora's Box

Here is the lid of Pandora's Box. What happened when it was opened?

This is the inside of the box. Write words about the story that start with each letter of "Hope." (This will make your poem.)

H _____

O _____

P _____

E _____

_____

# Standards

Students will

- Understand the defining features and structures of myths and historical fiction (McREL 13)

- Demonstrate a basic familiarity with a variety of classic fiction, folktales, and poetry (McREL 15)

- Appreciate literature and other creative expressions (AASL/AECT 5)

# Objectives

Students discuss plot and moral of the Pandora myth after hearing it. Students create an acrostic poem using the word "hope," which is the moral of the story.

# Directions

1. The library teacher reads or tells students the myth of Pandora's box. (If the source is too long, the teacher may simply tell the story.) This myth can be found in most mythology books (such as *A Children's Treasury of Mythology* by Bee Willey). It can also be found in the *Childcraft Encyclopedia.*

2. After reading or telling the story, the library teacher points out that mythology was created to explain how things on Earth came to be. The class should then discuss what happened when Pandora's box was opened. The class should also tell what was created when Pandora's box was opened (sadness and hope).

3. The class should think of some words associated with today's story that have the same initial letters as the letters in the word "hope." List those words on the board. Students will write those words in the bottom box of their worksheets, thus creating an acrostic poem.

4. The top box from the worksheet represents the lid of Pandora's box. The bottom box with the poem represents the inside of Pandora's box.

5. After students write the poem, they can cut out the top and bottom boxes. The top half of the box lid should be stapled to the top of the bottom box, making it look like a hinge. It will look like a paper box that opens to reveal "hope."

6. Students share their poems in language arts class.

# Learning Styles

Linguistic (writing), musical (rhythm of poetry), and interpersonal (working in groups)

# Teaching Team

Language arts and library teachers

# Suggested Resources

*Childcraft Encyclopedia: The How and Why Library.* Chicago: World Book, 2001.

Willey, Bee. *A Children's Treasury of Mythology.* New York: Barnes & Noble, 1994.

# Chapter 5

## Fourth-Grade Lesson Plans

In order to create solid professional-based library lesson plans, the following selected Kendall and Marzano or McREL National Education Standards and Benchmarks for Kindergarten were chosen from the area of language arts, as it directly correlates with library information and appreciation skills. Furthermore, the AASL (American Association of School Libraries) and the AECT (Association for Educational Communications and Technology) list of Information Literacy Standards were applied to every lesson to ensure that all students will develop literary appreciation and will be effective users of information and ideas (listed in the Introduction). Teaching objectives were also given for each lesson as linked to the standards or active goals. Finally, Gardner's multiple intelligences are also integrated into each lesson, as all students have different methods of learning (also listed in the Introduction).

*Each lesson plan has a direct reference to the following numbered McREL benchmarks under the corresponding standards, as well as a direct reference to AASL/AECT standards.* Finally, all of the following twenty-minute lesson plans should be used in conjunction with the other teachers whenever possible. Moreover, all lesson plans are not the only means, but some of many, for library instruction. The following lessons can provide whole group discussion ideas, or they can provide individual or small group worksheet work.

# Fourth-Grade Library Standards and Language Arts Benchmarks (McREL)*

Fourth-grade students will be able to

- Effectively gather and use information for research purposes (Standard 4)

    1. Use encyclopedias to gather information for research topics

    2. Use dictionaries to gather information for research topics

    3. Use key words, indexes, cross references, and letters on volumes to find information for research topics

    4. Use multiple representations of information (e.g., maps, charts) to find information for research topics

    5. Use the card catalog to locate books for research purposes (for grades 6–8)

- Demonstrate competence in general skills and strategies for reading literature (Standard 6)

    6. Become aware of the geographic information important to the stories one reads

    7. Share response with peers

    8. Identify the main characters in works containing only a few basic characters

    9. Recognize the basic elements of plot

- Demonstrate competence in the general skills and strategies for reading information (Standard 7)

    10. Use chapter and section headings, topic sentences, and summary sentences to construct main ideas

    11. Understand the uses of various parts of a book (index, table of contents, glossary, and appendix)

- Demonstrate competence in applying the reading process to specific types of literary texts (Standard 8)

    12. Understand the defining features and structures of fantasies, fables and fairy tales at this development level

    13. Understand the defining features of mysteries, realistic fiction, adventure stories, and humorous stories at this developmental level

    14. Understand the defining features and structures of myths and historical fiction at this developmental level

    15. Independently apply the reading process and strategies to biographies and autobiographies

- Demonstrate a familiarity with selected literary works of enduring quality (Standard 13)

    16. Demonstrate a familiarity with a variety of classic fiction, folktales, and poetry

    17. Demonstrate a familiarity with a variety of selected nonfiction

---

*Copyright 2000, McREL. Reprinted by permission of McREL.

# Which President Wore a Stovepipe Hat?

1. Find out something about President Lincoln. Use the book called *Lincoln: A Photobiography*. Look at the pictures in the book to answer these:

Find a picture of the president that surprised you.
What page is it on? _____
Why did you choose that picture? _____
_____
_____

2. Find a collective biography book to find out more about President Lincoln. (An example is *The Book of Presidents*.) Answer the following questions:

Where was Lincoln born? _____

How old was he when he became president? _____

Name one thing he did as a child. _____

What was one thing that he did when he was president? _____
_____

3. What makes a good president? Why? _____
_____
_____
_____
_____

## Standards

Students will

- Independently applies the reading process and strategies to biographies and autobiographies (McREL 15)
- Access information efficiently and effectively (AASL/AECT 1)
- Evaluate information critically and competently (AASL/AECT 2)
- Use information accurately and creatively (AASL/AECT 3)
- Recognize the importance of information to a democratic society (AASL/AECT 7)
- Participate effectively in groups to pursue and generate information (AASL/AECT 9)

## Objectives

Students learn about biographies and where to find them in the library. Small groups of students will search an individual photobiography and then collective biographies to answer worksheet questions regarding President Abraham Lincoln.

## Directions

1. Students search an individual biography and then a collective biography to find information about Lincoln. This may be a good activity for President's Day.

2. Before starting their president worksheets, the class reviews the definition of biography: Biographies are books about people's lives. Their call numbers begin with the letter B or the number 92. They are put on the shelf under the last name of the person about whom the book is written (a book about Christopher Columbus is shelved by Columbus). A collective biography is a collection of biographies of different persons' lives, usually with something in common (for example, a collective biography might focus on all the U.S. presidents or on African Americans). The library teacher then shows students where biographies are located in the library.

3. The teacher shows students where to find collective sources on presidents (such as Krull's *Lives of the Presidents*) and *Lincoln: A Photobiography* (this source is needed to complete the worksheet). Multiple copies of this title may be borrowed through interlibrary loan networks if desired.

4. Once students know where to find the required sources, groups of three work together to complete their president worksheets.

5. If there is time, students will share their worksheet answers.

6. The social studies teacher may have each student choose a presidential biography for reading and reporting.

## Learning Styles

Linguistic (reading and trivia) and interpersonal (group work)

## Teaching Team

Library and social studies teachers

## Suggested Resources

Freeman, Russell. *Lincoln: A Photobiography*. New York: Clarion Books, 1987.

Krull, Kathleen. *Lives of the Presidents*. San Diego, CA: Harcourt Brace, 1998.

# Mixed-Up Book Parts

Match the correct phrase with the book part.

| Book Part | Phrase |
|---|---|
| ___ Table of contents | A. definitions of words |
| ___ Title page | B. groups of pages that the book is divided into |
| ___ Spine label | C. mentions people who have helped out |
| ___ Cover | D. an alphabetical list of the books' subjects |
| ___ Copyright page | E. outside of the book |
| ___ Index | F. list of chapters in the book (located in front) |
| ___ Glossary | G. includes author, title, illustrator, publisher, and place of publishing |
| ___ Dedication page | H. the call number to tell where to find the book |
| ___ Chapters | I. page that shows when the book was published |

## Standards

Students will

- Understand the uses of various parts of a book (index, table of contents, glossary, and appendix) (McREL 11)

- Access information efficiently and effectively (AASL/AECT 1)

- Strive for excellence in information seeking (AASL/AECT 6)

## Objectives

Students discuss book parts. Small student groups review book parts. Individual students complete worksheets or quiz sheets on book parts.

## Directions

1. The library teacher can use the book parts sheet as either a worksheet or a quiz.

2. The class discusses the following book parts: the cover (the outside of a book), the spine label or call number (tells where to find the book), the title page (which includes the title, author, illustrator, publisher, and place of publishing), the copyright page (when a book was published), the dedication page (dedicates the book to someone important to the author), the table of contents (chapter lists), chapters (divisions within the book), the glossary (definition of words), and the index (subject lists). The library teacher should point out the importance of knowing book parts. For example, the glossary helps readers define words found in the book, the index provides readers with quick access to main topics in the book, the title and the copyright pages will provide information needed for a bibliography, and so on.

3. Class volunteers point out examples of book parts using library books.

4. Students break into small groups to identify book parts using library books. Students may time each other during their identification of book parts for a fun review.

5. Students will finally be ready to complete the book parts worksheet or quiz.

6. The language arts teachers could have students identify the book parts of a textbook.

## Learning Styles

Bodily kinesthetic (active), linguistic (writing), interpersonal, and intrapersonal learning skills

## Teaching Team

Language arts and library teachers

## Suggested Resources

Any books that contains the book parts discussed in the lesson.

# Fiction-Oh!

Oh! Which fiction will you read? 1. Choose and read a different kind of fiction from the board below. 2. When your book is read, you can cross off that square. Can you cross off all the squares?

## Standards

Students will

- Share response with peers (McREL 7)

- Understand the defining features of mysteries, realistic fiction, adventure stories, and humorous stories at this developmental level (McREL 13)

- Understand the defining features and structures of myths and historical fiction at this developmental level (McREL 14)

- Appreciate literature and other creative expressions (AASL/AECT 5)

## Objectives

Students become familiar with different genres. Students complete a genre game while reading fiction books.

## Directions

1. The library teacher explains genres and then holds a book talk on one or two books from different genres. (For example, the teacher could tell students about the book *Titanic Crossing*, noting that this book is historical fiction because the true story of the *Titanic* happened long ago.)

2. The library teacher describes other genres such as mystery (*Ghost Brother*), historical fiction (*Gone Away Lake*), adventure (*Far North*), humorous (*Wayside School*), sports fiction (*Million Dollar Shot*), science fiction (*McMummy*), realistic fiction (*Saving Shiloh,*), fantasy (*Catwings*), and others.

3. After the book talk, students will receive the Fiction-Oh! worksheet, which is similar to bingo. The language arts teacher could be in charge of this activity. The teacher explains that students should expand their reading and try to read different genres. When they read a different genre, they can cross off that square on their sheets. The middle square could be a free square for which students could read their choice of any school library book. Students may "play" the game for four to six weeks, or until they have crossed off three squares in a row.

4. Students may eventually book talk one of their Fiction-Oh! books in library class or in language arts class. Before giving the book talk, students should give the title, author, and genre. Students should be given the following simple rules for their book talks: (1) They should never tell the ending. (2) They should tell only the best parts. (3) The book talks should only take two or three minutes.

## Learning Styles

Linguistic (reading) and intrapersonal (working alone)

## Teaching Team

Language arts and library teachers

## Suggested Resources

Adler, C. S. *Ghost Brother*. New York: Clarion Books, 1990.

Byars, Betsy. *McMummy*. New York: Puffin Books, 1993.

Enright, Elizabeth. *Gone Away Lake*. San Diego, CA: Harcourt Brace Jovanovich, 1957.

Gutman, Dan. *Million Dollar Shot*. New York: Hyperpion, 1987.

Hobbs, Will. *Far North*. New York: William Morrow, 1996.

Le Guin, Ursula. *Catwings*. New York: Scholastic, 1990.

Naylor, Phyllis Reynolds. *Saving Shiloh*. New York: Scholastic, 1998.

Sachar, Louis. *Wayside School Is Falling Down*. New York: Econo-Clad Books, 1999.

Williams, Barbara. *Titanic Crossing*. New York: Dial Books for Young Readers, 1995.

# Card Catalog Types

Every book has a card catalog reference, which is a way to help you locate it in the library. These references are found in the card catalog. Can you tell what's different about each of these cards?

There are three kinds of cards:

1. Subject Card

2. Title Card

3. Author Card

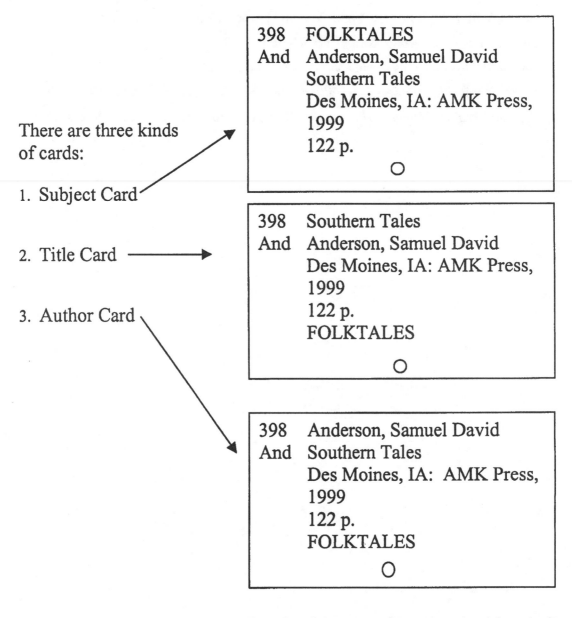

| 398 | FOLKTALES |
| And | Anderson, Samuel David |
| | Southern Tales |
| | Des Moines, IA: AMK Press, 1999 |
| | 122 p. |

| 398 | Southern Tales |
| And | Anderson, Samuel David |
| | Des Moines, IA: AMK Press, 1999 |
| | 122 p. |
| | FOLKTALES |

| 398 | Anderson, Samuel David |
| And | Southern Tales |
| | Des Moines, IA: AMK Press, 1999 |
| | 122 p. |
| | FOLKTALES |

Directions: Find an example of each of these card types using the card catalog: Subject Card ___    Author Card ____    Title Card ___

## Standards

Students will

- Use the card catalog to locate books for research purposes (McREL 5)
- Access information efficiently and effectively (AASL/AECT 1)
- Practice ethical behavior in regard to information and information technology (AASL/AECT 8)
- Participate effectively in groups to pursue and generate information (AASL/AECT 9)

## Objectives

Students discuss reasons for using different types of card catalog cards while using the automated or print catalog. Students distinguish the different cards. Students locate an example of each card type.

## Directions

1. The library teacher makes an overhead transparency and, if desired, student copies of the card catalog worksheet.

2. The library teacher shows students the different types of cards in a card catalog using the overhead transparency. The library teacher invites students to explain how the card types are different and then how they are alike. The teacher explains why choosing a search option (subject, author, title) makes a difference when using automated or print cards.

3. Small student groups find an example of each author, title, and subject card type using the automated or print card catalog. If using the automated catalog, students can print copies and then label each card type. If students are using print cards, they can lightly pencil in each card type on the card itself.

4. Card catalog types are easy, but can be complicated for some students. The library teacher has the class review card types before leaving the library.

5. The language arts teacher may ask students to review the card types in the main classroom. Perhaps students may use discarded library cards for classroom review.

## Learning Styles

Bodily kinesthetic (active), interpersonal (working together), and spatial (visual)

## Teaching Team

Language arts and library teachers

## Suggested Resources

Automated card catalog computer stations or card catalog stations.

# Dewey Decimal for Kids—The DDC Bee

Melvil Dewey created the Dewey decimal classification system (DDC). He decided that subjects should be grouped into ten basic categories. His system uses decimals. The Dewey decimal system is nonfiction!

| Categories | Examples Just For Kids: |
|---|---|
| 000s | General things, computers, encyclopedias |
| 100s | Way people think, the mind, feelings |
| 200s | Religion, the Bible |
| 300s | U.S. Constitution, fairy tales, holidays such as Christmas |
| 400s | The dictionary, foreign-language dictionaries |
| 500s | Space, weather, wild animals, plants, science things |
| 600s | Pets, food, jobs such as farming or teaching |
| 700s | Drawing books, music, sports |
| 800s | Poetry, jokes and other literature |
| 900s | History, American Indians, White House |

Here's a bookmark for your Dewey Decimal practice:

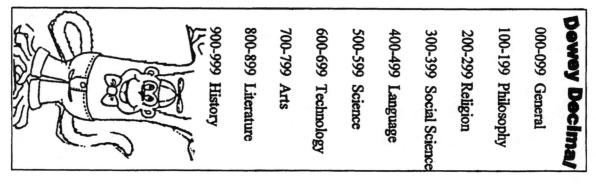

Go quickly to the library shelves to find books in each DDC (Dewey decimal category).

| Category | Title | Call Number |
|----------|-------|-------------|
| 000 | ------------------------------------------- | --------  -------- |
| 100 | ------------------------------------------- | --------  -------- |
| 200 | ------------------------------------------- | --------  -------- |
| 300 | ------------------------------------------- | --------  -------- |
| 400 | ------------------------------------------- | --------  -------- |
| 500 | ------------------------------------------- | --------  -------- |
| 600 | ------------------------------------------- | --------  -------- |
| 700 | ------------------------------------------- | --------  -------- |
| 800 | ------------------------------------------- | --------  -------- |
| 900 | ------------------------------------------- | --------  -------- |

## Standards

Students will

- Demonstrate a familiarity with selected nonfiction (McREL 17)
- Access information efficiently and effectively (AASL/AECT 1)
- Practice ethical behavior in regard to information and information technology (AASL/AECT 8)

## Objectives

Students will understand how to use the Dewey Decimal Classification System in order to better locate nonfiction books. Student pairs will write down book titles from each Dewey Decimal category classification on their worksheets.

## Directions

1. The library teacher makes an overhead transparency and student copies of the two lesson worksheets, Dewey Decimal for Kids and the DDC Bee.

2. The library teacher explains the Dewey Decimal System while using the Dewey Decimal for Kids transparency. The library teacher will show examples of different Dewey Decimal Classifications (DDC) within the library while emphasizing each major category.

3. Students complete the DDC Bee worksheet using the Dewey Decimal for Kids worksheet. Student pairs quickly locate examples of books within each of the ten Dewey Decimal categories.

4. To begin the activity, the teacher will assign student pairs to different nonfiction places to avoid congestion. The teacher tells students to work quickly and carefully. This activity may be timed to make it a fun, challenging learning activity.

5. If there is time, students may share completed worksheets with each other.

6. The Dewey Decimal bookmark on the worksheet may serve as a reminder of how the system works. Students may color their bookmarks.

7. Math students may visit the library at another time to further study the Dewey Decimal System. Math students may copy down book titles and their corresponding Dewey Decimal numbers. After compiling a small list of titles and call numbers, students may then read the titles with their decimal numbers, thus practicing how to read the numerical decimal degrees.

## Learning Styles

Mathematical (problem solving), linguistic (writing), and interpersonal learning

## Teaching Team

Library and mathematics teachers

## Suggested Resources

The nonfiction area of the library media center

# Myths

Elements of a myth are:
1. Gods and Goddesses who can be Greek, Roman, and others
2. Heroes that do amazing things
3. Battles of good and evil where good ways win
4. Monsters
5. Adventures

Read a story from a mythology book:

*King Midas and the Golden Touch*      *Tales of Pan*
*A Children's Treasury of Myth*       *Medusa*
*The Golden Hoard*                    *Procrustes*
*Theseus & the Minotaur*              *The Cyclopes*

Create a mythology cartoon strip after reading a myth like King Midas:

|  |  |  |  |
|--|--|--|--|
|  |  |  |  |

## Standards

Students will

- Recognize the basic elements of plot (McREL 9)
- Understand the defining features and structures of myths and historical fiction at this developmental level (McREL 14)
- Appreciate literature and other creative expressions (AASL/AECT 5)
- Recognize the importance of information to a democratic society (AASL/AECT 7)

## Objectives

Students relate the elements of a myth to the King Midas story after hearing it. Students create a mythology cartoon strip depicting a wish granted to them by a mythical creature.

## Directions

1. The library teacher guides a discussion concerning the elements of myths using an overhead transparency of the Myths worksheet and then hands out individual copies to students.

2. After discussing the elements of myths, the library teacher will read *King Midas and the Golden Touch*. (Charlotte Craft wrote an elementary version of *King Midas and the Golden Touch*.)

3. After hearing the myth, students relate the elements of myths to the King Midas tale.

4. Students use the mythology cartoon strip to depict what they would choose if a mythological creature promised to grant them one wish. They should come up with a title and an ending for their cartoons.

5. If there is time, the teacher can display other titles of myths found in the library.

6. The mythology video called *Jason and the Argonauts* would be an excellent language arts follow-up for the mythology lesson.

7. Social studies students can learn about ancient Greece with the *Encyclopedia Britannica* CD-ROM or *Britannica*.

## Learning Styles

Musical (music of the video), spatial (creating and drawing), intrapersonal (working alone), and linguistic (reading and writing)

## Teaching Team

Language arts, library, and social studies teachers

## Suggested Resources

Craft, Charlotte. *King Midas and the Golden Touch*. New York: Morrow Junior Books, 1999.

*Encyclopedia Britannica*. Chicago: Britannica, 2001 [CD-ROM].

*Encyclopedia Britannica* online: http://www .britannica.com

Fisher, Leonard Everett. *Thesus and the Minotaur*. New York: Holiday House, 1988.

Hutton, Warwick. *Odysseus and the Cyclops*. New York: McElderry Books, 1996.

*Jason and the Argonauts*. Culver City, CA: Columbia Tristar Home Videos, 2000 [DVD].

Lattimore, Deborah Nourse. *Medusa*. New York: HarperCollins, 2000.

Price, Margaret. *A Golden Hoard*. New York: Barnes & Noble, 1994.

Willey, Bee. *A Children's Treasury of Mythology*. New York: Barnes & Noble, 1994.

# Where Is the Main Idea?

**What is this paragraph trying to tell you?**

To discover the point of a paragraph, first find the topic sentence and then look at the rest of the sentences or summary sentences. Then you'll have the main idea! Look up an animal in the encyclopedia so that you can practice finding the main idea.

1. Which animal will you look up? _____

2. Which encyclopedia will you use? _____

3. Write a short paragraph about the animal from the encyclopedia.

_____

_____

_____

_____

_____

4. The topic sentence tells what the paragraph is all about. Circle it.

5. The rest of the sentences after the topic sentence are summary sentences. Put a square around the summary sentences.

6. What is the main idea? _____

## Standards

Students will

- Use encyclopedias to gather information for research topics (McREL 1)

- Use chapter and section headings, topic sentences, and summary sentences to construct main ideas (McREL 10)

- Access information efficiently and effectively (AASL/AECT 1)

- Evaluate information critically and competently (AASL/AECT 2)

- Practice ethical behavior in regard to information and information technology (AASL/AECT 8)

## Objectives

Students discuss the concept of the "main idea." Using an encyclopedia, students write down a paragraph about an animal. Students find the topic and summary sentence of the paragraph to locate the main idea.

## Directions

1. Finding the main idea is sometimes difficult for fourth graders.

2. The library teacher makes an overhead transparency and student copies of the main idea worksheet. The teacher also makes an overhead transparency of a brief paragraph from any informational source to use as an example.

3. The library teacher explains how to find the main idea: to find the main idea, students should look at the topic and summary sentences in informational books. The topic sentence states what the paragraph is about. The rest of the sentences in the paragraph are called the summary sentences.

4. After hearing how to find the main idea, the class looks at the teacher's transparency paragraph copy to find the main idea.

5. The class breaks into small groups to work on their Main Idea worksheets. They will find the main idea from an encyclopedia entry on a chosen animal. Students choose either a print or CD-ROM encyclopedia, such as *World Book Multimedia* CD-ROM or *World Book Encyclopedia*. Students should be reminded of copyright laws when writing their paragraphs.

6. If there is time, students should look at a second paragraph to find the main idea.

7. In the social studies or science classrooms, students may review the concept of main ideas by locating the main idea in their textbooks.

## Learning Styles

Linguistic (reading and writing), mathematical (thinking logically), and interpersonal (working with others)

## Teaching Team

Library, science, and social studies teachers

## Suggested Resources

Encyclopedias in print or on CD-ROM.

## Which Tale Is It?

This is from the tall tale called: _____

**Guess which tall tale exaggeration is really from the story!**

1.
_____

2. _____

3. _____

4.
_____

--------------------------------------------------------

# Which tale is it?

## Standards

Students will

- Demonstrate a basic familiarity with a variety of selected classic fiction, folktales, and poetry (McREL 16)

- Appreciate literature and other creative expressions (AASL/AECT 5)

## Objectives

Students discuss tall tales. Student groups read a tall tale. Students write three exaggerations from their tall tale on worksheets. Students add their own exaggeration to the worksheets. Students guess which exaggeration was made up.

## Directions

1. The library teacher has students review the elements of a folktale or tall tale. Such elements could be the fact that folktales are often created from stories of actual people who helped to shape our country. During the process of retelling folktales or tall tales, stories become more elaborate and thus exaggerated.

2. Small groups of students read a tall tale. (Students may choose a tall tale such as Kellogg's *Pecos Bill, Sally Ann Thunder Ann Whirlwind Crockett,* or *Mike Fink* or a story from *Classic American Folk Tales* as retold by Zorn.)

3. After reading the tall tale, students will write the title on the top half of the worksheet. They will then write three tall tale exaggerations on any of the four blanks from the top half of the worksheet that asks, "Guess which tall tale is really from the story!" Students will add one made-up exaggeration on one of the four blanks.

4. Students cut along the dotted line on the worksheet. The half sheet with the dog wagging his tail will be the cover sheet. The inside of the sheet will be the four exaggerations. The page halves will be stapled together.

5. Students should guess which exaggeration was made up from other students' tall tale sheets.

6. These sheets should also be displayed in order for other classes to guess which exaggerated parts were from the original tall tale and which part was made up. Students will enjoy playing the guessing game.

7. In language arts, students can view the *Paul Bunyan* video as a follow-up.

## Learning Styles

Linguistic (reading, telling stories, and writing), interpersonal (working in groups), and spatial (illustrating)

## Teaching Team

Language arts and library teachers

## Suggested Resources

Kellogg, Steven. *Mike Fink*. New York: William Morrow, 1992.

Kellogg, Steven. *Paul Bunyan and the Blue Ox*. New York: William Morrow, 1984.

Kellogg, Steven. *Pecos Bill*. New York: William Morrow, 1986.

Kellogg, Steven. *Sally Ann Thunder Ann Whirlwind Crockett*. New York: William Morrow, 1995.

*Paul Bunyan*. Lincoln, NE: Reading Rainbow, 1984 [video].

Zorn, Steven. *Classic American Folk Tales*. Philadelphia: Running Press, 1992.

# Global Travel with International Fairy Tales

Global Travel

The title of my foreign fairy tale: _____

My fairy tale is from the country of: _____

Here is a picture illustrating the plot of my foreign fairy tale:

Global Travel

The title of my foreign fairy tale is: _____

My fairy tale is from the country of: _____

Here is a picture illustrating the plot of my foreign fairy tale:

## Standards

Students will

- Understand the defining features and structures of fantasies, fables, and fairy tales at this developmental level (McREL 12)
- Become aware of geographic information important to the story one reads (McREL 6)
- Recognize basic elements such as plot (McREL 9)
- Appreciate literature and other creative expressions (AASL/AECT 5)

## Objectives

Students discuss the elements of fairy tales. Student pairs read international fairy tales. Students illustrate plot and answer two questions on their worksheets.

## Directions

1.  The class will discuss the elements of fairy tales while thinking up examples of a fairy tale, such as *Beauty and the Beast*. The following elements may be copied onto the board: (1) The story may start out with "Once upon a time." (2) The story may end with "They lived happily ever after." (3) There's usually magic in a fairy tale. (4) The main character may be a princess or a prince. (5) There's a struggle between good and bad in fairy tales where good usually wins.

2.  The library teacher shows the illustrations of a foreign fairy tale book while discussing it. The class thinks of the clothing, language, and other things that portrayed the country shown in the book. They will recognize plot, geographic location or setting, and other fairy tale elements of that tale.

3.  Student pairs read a chosen fairy tale from a different country. The library teacher makes sure there are enough fairy tale books from different countries for all the student pairs (note the list of suggested books at the bottom of this page). Some students may use the *Multicultural Tales* CD-ROM. The teacher also supplies each student pair with worksheets.

4.  After reading their foreign fairy tale, students answer the questions on their fairy tale worksheets and illustrate the plot.

5.  As a follow-up, the class may watch a foreign fairy tale video, such as *Fool of the World and the Flying Ship* in library or in language arts class.

## Learning Styles

Linguistic (reading), spatial (drawing), and interpersonal (group work)

## Teaching Team

Language arts and library teachers

## Suggested Resources

Esbensen, Barbara. *The Star Maiden*. Boston: Little, Brown, 1988.

*Fool of the World and the Flying Ship*. Chicago: Churchill, 1991 [video].

Grimm Brothers. *The Elves and the Shoemaker*. Mahwah, NJ: Troll, 1981.

Martin, Eva. *Tales of the Far North*. New York: Dial Books for Young Readers, 1988.

*Mufaro's Beautiful Daughters*. Chicago: Churchill, 1991 [video].

*Multicultural Tales*. Houston, TX: Great Waves Software, 1995 [CD-ROM].

Winthop, Elizabeth. *Vasilissa the Beautiful*. New York: HarperCollins, 1991.

Yep, Lawrence. *Dragon Prince: A Chinese Beauty and the Beast Tale*. New York: HarperCollins, 1999.

Zelinsky, Paul. *Rapunzel*. New York: Dutton Children's Books, 1997.

# What's the Difference Between Dictionaries?

1. What is the title of a picture dictionary? _____

2. What is the title of a foreign language dictionary?

_____

Use that dictionary and find out how to say good-bye: _____

3. How many words are found in the largest dictionary in the library? ____
   *Hint: The cover may tell you the number.*

4. How many different kinds of dictionaries can you find?  List them:

   1. _____

   2. _____

   3. _____

   4. _____

   5. _____

   6. _____

   7. _____

   8. _____

5. Define the word *combustion* from two different dictionaries. Compare!
   1st dictionary definition: _____

_____

_____

2nd dictionary definition: _____

_____

_____

# Standards

Students will

- Use dictionaries to gather information for research topics (McREL 2)
- Access information efficiently and effectively (AASL/AECT 1)
- Evaluate information critically and competently (AASL/AECT 2)
- Use information accurately and creatively (AASL/AECT 3)
- Participate effectively in groups to pursue and generate information (AASL/AECT 9)

# Objectives

Students discover differences among various dictionaries. Student pairs will define words from different dictionaries.

# Directions

1. The library teacher shows and briefly explains the differences in some of the library dictionaries. (For example, the teacher may explain that foreign language dictionaries are used to find foreign words, picture dictionaries are used to see pictures of words, bigger dictionaries or unabridged dictionaries are used to find thousands more words than other dictionaries, and so on.)

2. The library teacher shows the class where various dictionaries are located in the library. Dictionary worksheets will be distributed to students.

3. Pairs of students will look at various dictionaries in order to complete the dictionary worksheet.

4. If there is time, the class can discuss their worksheet answers.

5. In language arts class, students may examine *Merriam Webster's Dictionary for Kids* on CD-ROM.

6. A foreign language teacher may visit the library or main classroom to teach a few basic words from the foreign language picture dictionary.

# Learning Styles

Bodily kinesthetic (active), linguistic (reading and writing), and interpersonal skills (working with each other)

# Teaching Team

Foreign language, language arts, and library teachers

# Suggested Resources

*Let's Learn French Picture Dictionary*. Lincolnwood, IL: Passport Books, 1991.

*Let's Learn Spanish Picture Dictionary*. Lincolnwood, IL: Passport Books, 1991.

McIlwain, John, Editor. *Dorling Kindersley Children's Illustrated Dictionary*. New York: Dorling Kindersley, 1994.

*Merriam Webster's Dictionary for Kids*. Burlington, NJ: Franklin Electronic, 2001 [CD-ROM].

*Random House Webster's Unabridged Dictionary*. New York: Random House, 1998.

*Scholastic Children's Dictionary*. New York: Scholastic, 1996.

# What's Cooking with Fantasy?

Look at the ingredients (title, plot, and so on) to see how it all cooked up.

1. Fantasy story title:

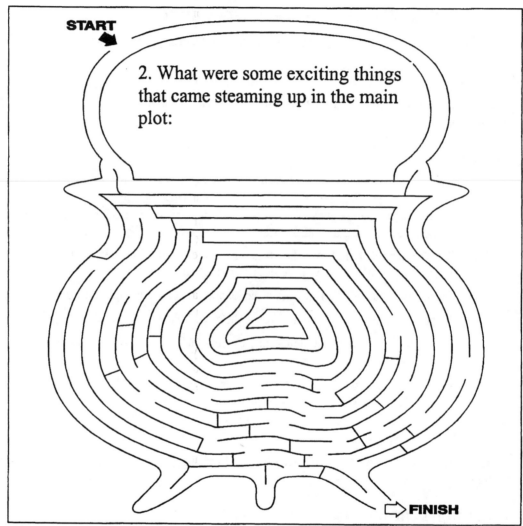

**START**

2. What were some exciting things that came steaming up in the main plot:

**FINISH**

The rest of the ingredients were the setting and the characters.
3. What's it all sitting on? What was the setting?
4. Who were the main characters that stirred up the action?

Now that you know all about the ingredients of your fantasy story, you can complete the fantasy kettle maze!

## Standards

Students will

- Share responses to literature with peers (McREL 7)
- Understand the defining features and structures of fantasies, fables, and fairy tales at this developmental level (McREL 12)
- Appreciate literature and other creative expressions (AASL/AECT 5)

## Objectives

After hearing a fantasy story, students discuss the elements of fantasy. Students explain and then write down fantasy title, plot, characters, and setting on worksheets. Students complete the worksheet maze.

## Directions

1. The library teacher explains that a fantasy is a story that has things in it that could never happen in real life, even though most of the story seems real.

2. The library teacher copies the fantasy worksheet for students. The teacher locates quick-reading fantasy stories. Carl Sandburg's collection of fantasy stories, *Rootabaga Stories,* would be a good source for this grade level. If multiple copies are not available, the teacher may read one fantasy story to the class.

3. After listening to or reading the fantasy, the class discusses what makes it a fantasy (things that sound real but could never really happen). They should also discuss the plot.

4. Students complete the list of ingredients for a good fantasy story on their fantasy cooking worksheets. They will write down the fantasy title followed by the main plot. They will then write down the setting and the main characters.

5. Students complete the fantasy kettle maze, if desired.

## Learning Styles

Linguistic (reading, writing, and telling stories) and spatial (imaginary)

## Teaching Team

Library teacher and others

## Suggested Resources

Sandburg, Carl. *Rootabaga Stories*. Bedford, MA: Applewood Books, 2001.

# Popping up with a Valentine Greeting

## Standards

Students will

- Demonstrate a familiarity with a variety of selected fiction, folktales, and poetry (McREL 16)
- Access information efficiently and effectively (AASL/AECT 1)
- Use information accurately and creatively (AASL/AECT 3)
- Appreciate literature and other creative expressions (AASL/AECT 5)

## Objectives

Students research the 800 section in the library to find jokes or poems for valentine greeting cards. Students create valentine note cards using those jokes or poems.

## Directions

1. Students use the valentine worksheet to make note cards for this activity. It may be copied onto pink or red paper.
2. Valentine's Day is a great opportunity to use the poetry section of the library. The teacher reads some brief Valentine's Day poems to the class. (A great Valentine's Day poetry book is *It's Valentine's Day* by Jack Prelutsky. The teacher may also read some jokes or riddles from the *Great Book of Riddles and Jokes* by Joseph Rosenbloom.)
3. After listening to a couple of Valentine's Day poems, jokes, or riddles, the teacher points out the poetry, joke, and riddle section of the library so that students may find other poems, jokes, or riddles.
4. Students will find and copy a short poem, joke, or riddle on the valentine note cards.
5. Once written, the note card should be folded in half, with the student poems or jokes written inside of it.
6. The students may decorate the cards and then give them away. The cards may be decorated in art class.

## Learning Styles

Spatial (create with art), linguistic (reading), musical (rhythm of poetry), and bodily kinesthetic (moving around to find sources)

## Teaching Team

Art and library teachers

## Suggested Resources

Prelutsky, Jack. *It's Valentine's Day*. New York: Econo-Clad Books, 1999.

Rosenbloom, Joseph. *Great Book of Riddles and Jokes*. New York: Sterling, 1999.

# Fiction or Nonfiction?

How can you tell if a book is true or make believe? Call numbers help!
<u>Nonfiction</u> call numbers have numbers along with other letters. Nonfiction is true.

<u>Fiction</u> is not true. Fiction has the letters "Fic" or just the letter "F" on the spine.

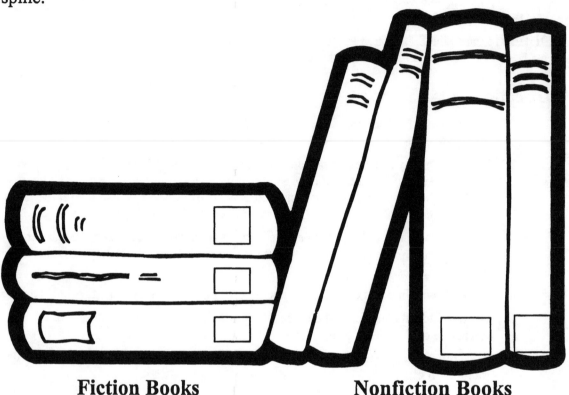

**Fiction Books**          **Nonfiction Books**

**Fiction Books**
1. Use the card catalog to find two fiction books.
2. Put each call number on a fiction book spine above. Then put each title on the spine.

**Nonfiction Books**
3. Now use the card catalog to find two nonfiction books.
4. Put each nonfiction call number on a book spine above. Then put each title on the spine.

## Standards

Students will

- Use the card catalog to locate books for research purposes (McREL 5)

- Access information efficiently and competently (AASL/AECT 1)

- Strive for excellence in information seeking (AASL/AECT 6)

- Practice ethical behavior in regard to information and information technology (AASL/AECT 8)

- Participate effectively in groups to pursue and generate information (AASL/AECT 9)

## Objectives

Students discuss the differences between nonfiction and fiction books. Small student groups locate two fiction and two nonfiction books from the card catalog. Students write the fiction and nonfiction call numbers and book titles on the worksheet books.

## Directions

1. The library teacher gives students the fiction and nonfiction worksheets to use in conjunction with the (automated) card catalog for this lesson. The teacher will use an overhead transparency copy of the worksheet.

2. First, the library teacher reads the top of the worksheet to explain that fiction books have "Fic" or the letter "F" on the spine. The teacher also explains that nonfiction books have numbers on the spine. Finally, the teacher reminds students that fiction is false, while nonfiction is true and has numbered call numbers.

3. The library teacher uses the overhead transparency to provide an example of how the students will complete their worksheets: students will find two fiction and two nonfiction books from the automated or print card catalog. Students will write their two fiction call numbers and titles on two of the three horizontal book drawings and will write the two nonfiction call numbers and titles on two of the four vertical book drawings on the worksheet.

4. Once students understand how to complete the worksheets, small groups complete the sheets.

5. If there is time, students share their completed worksheet responses.

## Learning Styles

Linguistic (reading and writing) and interpersonal (group work)

## Teaching Team

Library teacher and others if desired

## Suggested Resources

The library card catalog (automated or print).

# Be a Sport!

Your name _____        Your Sport _____

I. Complete the following bibliographical information about your book:
Title of your nonfiction sports book _____
Author _____
Publisher _____ Copyright _____
Place Published _____

II.  Fill in the blanks from the information you found in your book.
1.  What kind of equipment is used to play your sport?
_____
_____
_____

2.  As you look in your book, find, and then list the names of some famous athletes who play your sport.
_____
_____

III. Stop and use an electronic encyclopedia to find five more facts about your sport.
1. _____
2. _____
3. _____
4. _____
5. _____

IV.  What is your opinion about this sport?
_____

## Standards

Students will

- Use encyclopedias to gather information for research topics (McREL 1)
- Use the card catalog to locate books for research purposes (McREL 5)
- Demonstrate a familiarity with a variety of selected nonfiction (McREL 17)
- Access information efficiently and effectively (AASL/AECT 1)
- Evaluate information critically and competently (AASL/AECT 2)
- Pursue information related to personal interest (AASL/AECT 4)
- Strive for excellence in information seeking (AASL/AECT 6)

## Objectives

Student pairs select a sport after searching the card catalog for nonfiction sport resources. Students locate and write information from a nonfiction book and from the encyclopedia CD-ROM. Students also state their opinion about the sport.

## Directions

1. The physical education teacher may want to team teach this lesson with the library teacher.

2. Student pairs choose a sport after browsing through the automated card catalog for a non-fiction book on their chosen sport. The library teacher reminds students how to use the automated card catalog because some students may have forgotten.

3. After finding a nonfiction book on their chosen sport, student pairs will begin researching as guided by their worksheets. Students answer questions about their sport using their nonfiction books and the electronic or CD-ROM encyclopedia. They may use the *World Book Multimedia* CD-ROM or the *Encarta* CD-ROM encyclopedias.

4. Students express their opinions about their sports to instill critical thinking skills.

5. Students may present their reports in physical education class.

## Learning Styles

Linguistic (reading and writing), intrapersonal (working alone), and mathematical (computer)

## Teaching Team

Library and physical education teachers

## Suggested Resources

The card catalog, nonfiction books, and the following encyclopedias:

http://www.britannica.com

*Microsoft Encarta Encyclopedia Deluxe 2001*. Richmond, WA: Microsoft, 2001 [CD-ROM].

*World Book 2001 Multimedia Deluxe*. Chicago: World Book, 2001 [CD-ROM].

# Key Word Searching

Find the key word(s) to unlock the questions: (1) Read the question. (2) Select the key word(s). (3) Use the encyclopedia to look up your key word(s). (4) Find the answer. (5) Write down your key word(s) and the answer.

1. Where was President Bill Clinton born? _____
   What was the key word(s)? _____

2. How long does the wolf fish get? _____
   What was the key word(s)? _____

3. What is another name for porcupine fish? _____
   What was the key word(s)? _____

4. What was James Madison's famous job? _____
   What was the key word(s)? _____

5. What did Henry Ford manufacture? _____
   What was the key word(s)? _____

*Challenge Question:
Which three states are known for their dairy or milk cattle?
The three states are _____ .
What was the key word(s)? _____

## Standards

Students will

- Use encyclopedias to gather information for research topics (McREL 1)
- Use the key words, indexes, cross-references, and letters on volumes to find information for research topics (McREL 3)
- Access information efficiently and effectively (AASL/AECT 1)
- Evaluate information critically and competently (AASL/AECT 2)
- Use information accurately and creatively (AASL/AECT 3)
- Strive for excellence in information seeking (AASL/AECT 6)

## Objectives

The class reviews the use of key words for finding information in encyclopedias. Students think of questions and then come up with key words to search for the answers using encyclopedias.

## Directions

1. Since students often have a difficult time remembering how to use key words to search a topic, this lesson will benefit them. The key word worksheet could be used as an overhead or copied for student worksheets.

2. The library teacher reviews the fact that key words are used to find topics, subjects, or articles. For instance, when students need to find information about the birthplace of President Washington, they look up "Washington, George" (not "birthplace"). The key words are Washington, George.

3. The teacher prepares the class by having students think of questions that could be answered using the encyclopedia. As a group, students think of questions that could be answered using the encyclopedia. The teacher repeats two or three of their questions and asks students for the key word. The teacher looks up the key words to see if they will produce an answer. If that search is not successful, students provide another key word. The class repeats this activity until most students feel comfortable with key word searching.

4. Finally, paired or individual students will answer the key word worksheets.

5. Completed worksheet answers may be discussed in a whole-group setting.

6. To reinforce the concept of key words, students may look at chapter-end questions in their social studies textbooks. The social studies teacher may have students locate key words in the chapter questions, before answering the questions.

## Learning Styles

Bodily kinesthetic (active), linguistic (reading and writing), and mathematical (computer)

## Teaching Team

Library and social studies teachers

## Suggested Resources

Encyclopedias and social studies texts.

# Fourth-Grade Team Atlas Challenge

## Teacher's Copy

Divide students into teams according to the amount of available *Rand McNally Road Atlas and Travel Guides of the United States*. Distribute the atlases and begin the challenge! Ask teams the following questions. Fourth-grade students may need some hints.

Q1. Find the great lake that is closest to New York City. (*Searching hint:* find New York City.) *A: Lake Erie*

Q2. If I wanted to see the Chicago Bulls basketball team play a home game, how far would I have to travel from Des Moines, Iowa, to Chicago, Illinois? (*Searching hint:* Think of miles. Use the chart on mileage.) *A: 327 miles.*

Q3. Let's say I want to see a real alligator. What are the coordinates (or latitude and longitude lines) for the Everglades in Florida? (*Searching hint:* Look at the state of Florida.) *A: 5-6*

Q4. Which theme or amusement park is in Minnesota? (*Searching hint:* Look at the theme-park chart.) *A: Valley Fair*

Q5. Name an interstate that travels through New Orleans, Louisiana. (Searching hint: Louisiana is a state.) *A: Interstate 10*

Q6. What is the average temperature in Des Moines, Iowa, in the winter? (*Searching hint:* Look at the climate chart.) *A: 31.15*

Q7. What are the coordinates for Niagara Falls City, New York? (*Searching hint:* Look at the state of New York.) *A: E-3*

## Standards

Students will

- Use multiple representations of information (e.g., maps, charts) to find information for research topics (McREL 4)
- Access information efficiently and effectively (AASL/AECT 1)
- Recognize the importance of information to a democratic society (AASL/AECT 7)

## Objectives

Students find informational items in an atlas. Student teams compete to find the most correct answers by searching an atlas.

## Directions

1. The library teacher tells students that an atlas has maps, charts, pictures, and information relating to geography. The teacher explains that an atlas provides information for research topics when referring to the location of places. The library teacher shows students the different types of atlases that are available in the library.

2. To learn about the variety of things that are available in an atlas, the teacher uses an atlas similar to the *Rand McNally Road Atlas and Travel Guide of the United States*. The library teacher shows students that this atlas has a variety of geographic data, such as charts showing mileage from one city to another, climates, amusement park locations, and other information, along with maps of each state.

3. The teacher reminds students that coordinates are the grid lines of latitude and longitude, or the alphabetical and numerical lines found on the sides of maps. The teacher should show students these lines while talking.

4. Students compete in the Atlas Team Challenge. Students will form teams in ratio to the number of available atlases. Student teams could think of team names.

5. After teams have received their atlases, the library teacher starts the team challenge by asking the questions found on the teacher's worksheet. Note that separate student worksheets are provided for in this activity.

6. As teams locate the answers, a student will keep track of the correct answers on the board.

7. Students may continue to review atlases in social studies class. Team members may find atlas questions to ask of one another.

## Learning Styles

Linguistic (reading maps), spatial (reading charts and maps), and interpersonal (group work)

## Teaching Team

Library and social studies teachers

## Suggested Resources

*Rand McNally Road Atlas and Travel Guides of the United States*. Chicago: Rand McNally, 1997.

# My Story Scrapbook

By _____

---

My Scrapbook

My trip to _____
  (Book title)
With _____
  (Author)

p.1

---

My First Main Event          p.2

---

Geographic Location     p.3

---

Another Travel Event      p.4

---

Who I Met (Main Characters)   p.5

---

The Main Event (Plot)      p.6

## Standards

Students will

- Identify the main characters in works containing only a few basic characters (McREL 8)
- Recognize the basic elements of plot (McREL 9)
- Become aware of the geographic information important to the stories one reads (McREL 6)
- Understand the defining features and structures of myths and historical fiction at this developmental level (McREL 14)
- Appreciate literature and other creative expressions (AASL/AECT 5)

## Objectives

Students will hear a short fiction book. Students will illustrate plot, location, and main characters on their scrapbook-like worksheets.

## Directions

1.  The library media teacher provides students with copies of the scrapbook worksheet.

2.  The teacher reads a historical novella to the class. Fourth-grade students enjoy hearing *Bess's Log Cabin Quilt* by Anne Love. The teacher explains that scrapbooks are often made after a person has taken a trip. Such a scrapbook has pictures, mementos, and written descriptions of the trip. Students learn that hearing a story is like traveling through a book.

3.  As the students listen to the book, they will fill out the worksheet. Hearing a story is like actually traveling through a book or like going on a trip with it.

4.  The teacher reads up to a certain point in the story and then has the class illustrate one or two squares of their worksheet. The teacher may give students the option of illustrating or writing about their travels.

5.  After the teacher finishes reading the book, the class will discuss the events of their trip.

6.  The social studies teacher may wish to have students research the story's history and then create a time line of noteworthy historical events.

## Learning Styles

Linguistic (writing), interpersonal (working with others), and spatial (drawing)

## Teaching Team

Library and social studies teachers

## Suggested Resources

Love, Anne D. *Bess's Log Cabin Quilt*. New York: Holiday House, 1995.

Paulsen, Gary. *Nightjohn*. New York: Delacorte Press, 1993.

# What's on a Card Catalog Card?

---

977.77    Van Raden, Sarah and Rachel
Van       Fields of Opportunities
          Emily Van Raden, Ill
          Chicago: Gate Publishing, 1999
          122 p., illus
           The places to visit in Iowa.

          IOWA

---

Can you find the following items on the catalog card?

| | |
|---|---|
| Title | Copyright Date |
| Call Number | Author (s) |
| Publisher | Pages |
| Summary | Subject |
| Place Published | Illustrator |

Look at two catalog cards and decode the following information.

--------------------------------------------------------------------------------

## Fiction Book - Card 1

Call Number (left corner): _____

_____

Author: _____   Title of the book: _____

Illustrator: _____

Where published: _____   Publisher: _____

Copyright date: _____   Number of pages: _____

--------------------------------------------------------------------------------

## Nonfiction Book - Card 2

Call Number (left corner): _____

_____

Author: _____   Title of the book: _____

Illustrator: _____

Where published: _____   Publisher: _____

Copyright date: _____   Number of pages: _____

## Standards

Students will

- Use the card catalog to locate books for research purposes (McREL 5)
- Access information efficiently and effectively (AASL/AECT 1)
- Practice ethical behavior in regard to information and information technology (AASL/AECT 8)
- Participate effectively in groups to pursue and generate information (AASL/AECT 9)

## Objectives

Students learn how to find information on card catalog entries. The class completes a transparency worksheet on card catalog parts. Student groups use the automated card catalog to find a fiction and then a nonfiction book.

## Directions

1. The library teacher makes multiple copies of the Decoding a Card Catalog Card worksheet and an overhead transparency of the What's on a Card Catalog Card? worksheet.

2. It is crucial for students to be able to locate information on card catalog cards so that they can find all library sources quickly and efficiently.

3. To introduce this activity, the library teacher works with the class to complete the What's on a Card Catalog Card worksheet transparency as a group.

4. Small student groups will use the card catalog to complete their Decoding a Card Catalog Card worksheets. (If the library is not automated, students may use discarded catalog cards.) The groups of students will complete the section of their worksheets for fiction books first and then the nonfiction section.

5. If there is time, students may decode more catalog cards.

6. Students pairs may practice decoding more cards in the language arts classroom using discarded cards.

## Learning Styles

Bodily kinesthetic (active), spatial (visuals), and linguistic (writing)

## Teaching Team

Language arts and library teachers

## Suggested Resources

An overhead transparency or computer projection device and the automated card catalog or discarded catalog cards.

# Chapter 6

## Fifth-Grade Lesson Plans

In order to create solid professional-based library lesson plans, the following selected Kendall and Marzano or McREL National Education Standards and Benchmarks for Kindergarten were chosen from the area of language arts, as it directly correlates with library information and appreciation skills. Furthermore, the AASL (American Association of School Libraries) and the AECT (Association for Educational Communications and Technology) list of Information Literacy Standards were applied to every lesson to ensure that all students will develop literary appreciation and will be effective users of information and ideas (listed in the Introduction). Teaching objectives were also given for each lesson as linked to the standards or active goals. Finally, Gardner's multiple intelligences are also integrated into each lesson, as all students have different methods of learning (also listed in the Introduction).

*Each lesson plan has a direct reference to the following numbered McREL benchmarks under the corresponding standards, as well as a direct reference to AASL/AECT standards.* Finally, all of the following twenty-minute lesson plans should be used in conjunction with the other teachers whenever possible. Moreover, all lesson plans are not the only means, but some of many, for library instruction. The following lessons can provide whole group discussion ideas, or they can provide individual or small group worksheet work.

217

# Fifth-Grade Library Standards and Language Arts Benchmarks (McREL)*

Fifth-grade students will be able to

- Effectively gather and use information for research purposes (Standard 4)

    1. Use encyclopedias to gather information for research topics

    2. Use dictionaries to gather information for research topics

    3. Use key words, indexes, cross-references, and letters on volumes to find information for research topics

    4. Use multiple representations of information (e.g., maps, charts) to find information for research topics

    5. Use the *Reader's Guide to Periodical Literature* and other indexes to gather information (for grades 6–8)

    6. Use the card catalog to locate books for research purposes (for grades 6–8)

    7. Use a computer catalog to gather information for research purposes (for grades 6–8)

    8. Gather information for research topics using note taking (for grades 6–8)

    9. Understand the concept of a "likely informant" for obtaining information about a specific topic

- Demonstrate competence in general skills and strategies for reading literature (Standard 6)

    10. Become aware of the geographic information important to the story one reads

    11. Share responses to literature with peers

    12. Identify the main characters in works containing only a few basic characters

    13. Explain how characters or simple events in a work are like people or events in one's own life

    14. Recognize basic elements of plot

- Demonstrate competence in the general skills and strategies for reading information (Standard 7)

    15. Use chapter and section headings, topic sentences, and summary sentences to construct the main idea

    16. Understand the uses of the various parts of a book (index, table of contents, glossary, appendix)

- Demonstrate competence in applying the reading process to specific types of literary texts (Standard 8)

    17. Understand the defining features and structures of fantasies, fables, and fairy tales at this developmental level

    18. Understand the defining features and structures of mysteries, realistic fiction, historical fiction, adventure stories and humorous stories at this developmental level

    19. Understand the defining features and structures of myths at this developmental level

*Copyright 2000, McREL. Reprinted by permission of McREL.

20. Understand the defining features and structures of biographies and autobiographies at this developmental level

- Demonstrate a familiarity with selected literary works of enduring quality (Standard 13)

21. Demonstrate a basic familiarity with the characters and plots in selected mythology (e.g., Norse mythology, classical Greek)

22. Demonstrate a basic familiarity with a variety of selected classic fiction, folktales, and poetry

23. Demonstrate a familiarity with a variety of selected nonfiction

# Card Catalog Quiz

Name _____

Fill in the blanks in the sentences below from this word bank:

| | | | | |
|---|---|---|---|---|
| title | title card | subject card | author card | author |
| copyright | author | call number | illustrator | not true |
| publisher | subject | publishing place | title card | true pages |

1. If the title of the book is the first thing listed on a card catalog entry, it is called a _____ _____.

2. On an author card, the _____ is the first thing listed on a card catalog entry.

3. Automated card catalog searches can be accomplished by looking under a title, an author, or a _____.

4. Nonfiction books are true or not true? _____

5. When you are searching the card catalog, you should use the word "A," "An," or "The" if it is the first word of the title.  True or false? _____

6. Name the three main kinds of card catalog card entries:
1. _____          2. _____
3. _____

7.  List eight things found on a card catalog card entry:
1. _____          2. _____
3. _____          4. _____
5. _____          6. _____
7. _____          8. _____

## Standards

Students will

- Use the card catalog to locate books for research purposes (McREL 6)
- Access information efficiently and effectively (AASL/AECT 1)
- Strive for excellence in information seeking (AASL/AECT 6)

## Objectives

Students review card catalog parts while using the automated card catalog or print catalog cards. The teacher quizzes students on card catalog parts.

## Directions

1. The library teacher will reinforce the student skills of using the card catalog by having students review and then be quizzed over the card catalog. First, students need a review to prepare them. The language arts teacher may want to team teach this lesson with the library teacher.

2. The class should review the topic as a group. The following information should be listed on the board:
   A card catalog card includes a book's title, author, call number, copyright date, illustrator, number of pages, publisher and its location, and so on.

   The three main card catalog types are title, subject, and author cards.

   Never use the beginning title words of "A, An, or The" when they are the first words of a title. Nonfiction books are true.

3. After reviewing as a group, the class should break into smaller groups to review once more. The language arts and library teachers will check small groups for card catalog understanding.

4. When small student groups review for their quiz, they should first ask each other questions concerning what the class has just discussed. Secondly, they will review by looking at actual card catalog entries on the automated card catalog or with print card entries in order to identify card parts.

5. Once students feel comfortable with their review, they will take the quiz.

## Learning Styles

Linguistic (reading and writing) and interpersonal (group work)

## Teaching Team

Language arts and library teachers

## Suggested Resources

Automated card catalog entries on multiple computer stations or multiple print card catalog cards.

# Checking Through the Encyclopedia

Checking something out in the encyclopedia can go quickly with cross-reference words and key words. <u>Key words</u> are the subjects or titles of an article, which point directly to your information. <u>Cross-reference</u> words point you to other places to find information. Cross-reference code words are "See" or "See also."

Look up these encyclopedia key words. Find the cross-reference words.

1. Key word: Comets
   Write one cross-reference word for Comets: _____

2. Key word: Dog
   Write two cross-reference words for Dog:

   _____     _____

3. Key word: Cobra
   Write one cross-reference word for Cobra: _____

4. Key word: Technology
   Write two cross-reference words for Technology:

   _____     _____

5. Key word: Football
   Write one cross-reference word for Football: _____

6. Look up one of the cross-reference words. Write ten brief facts:

# Standards

Students will

- Use key words, indexes, cross references, and letters on volumes to find information for research topics (McREL 3)

- Access information efficiently and effectively (AASL/AECT 1)

# Objectives

Students review key words and cross-references. Students will locate cross-referenced words in encyclopedias. Students will locate ten brief facts about one of their cross-referenced words.

# Directions

1. Since students have a difficult time recalling cross-referenced and key words, this lesson reviews those terms. The library teacher makes an overhead transparency and student copies of the encyclopedia worksheet.

2. The library teacher supplies two or more encyclopedia sets for this lesson. If multiple encyclopedia volumes are not an option, small groups or pairs of students should work together.

3. The library teacher reviews key word and cross-referenced word searching using the transparency.

4. Following the review, students complete the worksheet.

5. Once students have found all of their cross-references, they will select one of their cross-referenced words in order to find ten brief facts.

6. For a follow-up, the language arts teacher may have students locate cross-referenced words in classroom encyclopedias.

# Learning Styles

Linguistic (reading), interpersonal (working together), and bodily kinesthetic (active researching)

# Teaching Team

Language arts and library teachers

# Suggested Resources

Any encyclopedias.

# Chinese Fables

Read a Chinese fable from a book, such as *A Chinese Zoo* by Demi.
Then write a haiku poem about the fable on the fan.

## Standards

Students will

- Understand the defining features and structures of fantasies, fables, and fairy tales at this developmental level (McREL 17)
- Demonstrate a basic familiarity with a variety of selected classic fiction, folktales, and poetry (McREL 22)
- Appreciate literature and other creative expressions (AASL/AECT 5)

## Objectives

Students listen to a Chinese fable after reviewing fable elements. Students will create a haiku poem regarding the plot of their Chinese fable.

## Directions

1. The language arts teacher may want to teach students how to write haiku poems before library class.
2. The library teacher locates Chinese fables, such as the ones found in the Chinese fable book *A Chinese Zoo,* adapted by Demi. The library teacher reads a fable to the class.
3. Before hearing the fable, the library class reviews the elements of fables. Such elements are that fables are often about talking animals and have a moral or lesson to be learned.
4. After listening to the Chinese fable(s), students create a haiku poem about the plot. The library teacher reminds students that haiku is a three-line form of poetry. The first line has five syllables, the second line has seven, and the third line has five syllables. (Even though haiku is Japanese and not Chinese, students will enjoy creating an Asian poem.)
5. Students will write their poems on the fan worksheet. They may decorate their paper fan worksheets. If the worksheet is reproduced on stiff paper so that the fan may be used, the art teacher may want to help students paint decorations on the fans in art class.
6. If time permits, students may share their haiku poems.

## Learning Styles

Interpersonal (group work), linguistic (reading, telling stories, writing), spatial (decorating and illustrating), and musical (rhythm of poetry)

## Teaching Team

Art, language arts, and library teachers

## Suggested Resources

Demi. *A Chinese Zoo*. San Diego, CA: Harcourt Brace Jovanovich, 1987.

## Where Are the Book Parts?

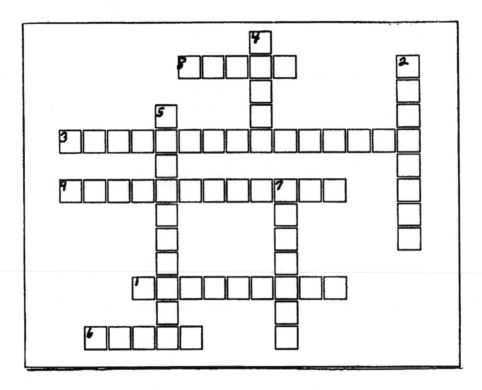

Find the book parts. Fill in the missing book part on the puzzle.

1. The _____ has the title, author, publisher, place of publication, and illustrator.
2. The _____ defines words.
3. The page that has the chapters listed is the _____.
4. A left-hand page is called a _____.
5. The _____ page dedicates the book to a person or persons.
6. The backbone of the book that has the call numbers is the _____.
7. The _____ is the introduction to the book.
8. The list of subjects and their page numbers is the _____.
9. The list of books to find more information is the _____.

## Standards

Students will

- Understand the uses of the various parts of a book (McREL 16)
- Access information efficiently and effectively (AASL/AECT 1)
- Strive for excellence in information seeking (AASL/AECT 6)

## Objectives

Students discuss and demonstrate book parts. Students complete a book parts puzzle worksheet.

## Directions

1.  The teacher provides copies of the book parts puzzle worksheet for student use.

2.  The library teacher writes a list of the book parts on the library board including the spine, title page, table of contents, dedication page, copyright page, glossary, preface or foreword, bibliography, and index. The teacher explains that left-hand pages are called the verso, and right-hand pages are called the recto. He or she may choose to leave this list of words on the board as a word bank for the book parts puzzle.

3.  The class discusses the book parts, and student volunteers show examples of each from books on the shelf. As students display the book parts, the teacher helps the class give the definition and purpose of those parts. For example, the spine is the backbone of a book; the title page displays the author, title, illustrator, publisher, and place of publication; the copyright page is the back of the title page and provides copyright information; the dedication page dedicates the book to a person or persons; the table of contents provides a chapter list; the preface or foreword provides an introduction; the glossary provides word definitions); the bibliography is a list of sources used to write the book; and the index is a list of subjects with their page numbers.

4.  Once students have learned these definitions, they will answer their worksheet questions by filling in the correct book part answers on the puzzle blanks. Leaving the discussion words on the board provides a word bank for assistance.

5.  In language arts class, students may find book parts of other books for a further reinforcement of book parts.

## Learning Styles

Linguistic (reading and writing), intrapersonal (working alone), and bodily kinesthetic (being active)

## Teaching Team

Language arts and library teachers

## Suggested Resources

Any books that contains the book parts listed on the worksheet.

# Looking at Our Country

**Gazetteer or Geographic Dictionary** - used for descriptions of countries, cities, rivers, mountains, and other places to answer these:

1. What are the square miles for Claire Lake? _____

2. List the places that have the same name as the town of Clarion: _____
_____

3. What states have the county named Wright County? _____
_____

4. What is the population of New York City, New York? _____

5. Look up the Catskill Mountains. Describe it: _____
_____

**Atlases** – used for cities, states, or counties (political atlas) and used for natural things like rivers and mountains(physical atlas) to answer these:

1. What is the mileage from the city of Des Moines to the city of Denver. The miles are : _____ (try a political map)

2. Find the map coordinates (longitude or latitude) for the city of Dallas, Texas. The map coordinates are: _____

3. Write the names of the Great Lakes:

_____
_____

## Standards

Students will

- Use multiple representations of information (e.g., maps, charts) to find information for research topics (McREL 4)

- Use dictionaries to gather information for research topics (McREL 2)

- Access information efficiently and effectively (AASL/AECT 1)

- Evaluate information critically and competently (AASL/AECT 2)

- Use information accurately and creatively (AASL/AECT 3)

- Participate effectively in groups to pursue and generate information (AASL/AECT 9)

## Objectives

Students discuss the purposes of geographic dictionaries, gazetteers, political atlases, and physical atlases. Student groups complete the geographic worksheets using geographic dictionaries, gazetteers, and atlases.

## Directions

1. The library teacher shows the geographic dictionary or gazetteer and explains how to use this source. (For example, a gazetteer or geographic dictionary is used to find names, country descriptions, cities, rivers, mountains, counties, and other geographic features of our world.)

2. The teacher points out and explains the purposes of political and physical atlases. The political atlas shows manmade boundaries of states, cities, and counties. The physical atlas includes maps that show the natural features of our land, such as rivers and mountains.

3. The teacher should have at least two copies of each atlas and gazetteer available.

4. The teacher provides students with the worksheet and assigns them to groups according to the number of available resources.

5. Small groups of students will then need to research different geographic aspects of the United States from the atlases and the gazetteer.

6. To avoid congestion at first, groups may be appointed a different worksheet question.

7. If groups complete their worksheets early, they should browse through different atlases to find facts for small-group sharing.

8. Students may locate places with a physical print map or with the *Animated Atlas* CD-ROM computerized map in their social studies classroom.

## Learning Styles

Mathematical (logical thinking), interpersonal (working together), and linguistic (reading)

## Teaching Team

Library and social studies teachers

## Suggested Resources

*Animated Atlas* (Animated Reference Library). Chicago: Clearvue, 1997 [CD-ROM].

Espenshade, Edward, editor. *Goode's World Atlas*. Chicago: Rand McNally, 1990.

*Merriam Webster's Geographic Dictionary*. Springfield, MA: Merriam Webster, 1997.

*Rand McNally Premier World Atlas*. Chicago: Rand McNally, 1998.

*Rand McNally Road Atlas and Travel Guides of the United States*. Chicago: Rand McNally, 1997.

# Putting a Finger on the *Readers' Guide*

**Directions:** Read the following sample of an entry from the *Readers' Guide to Periodical Literature* and decode it for the Periodical Call Slip.

**Sample Entry:**

> **BASKETBALL**
> Basketball Heights.  Adam Keeling. il. *Sports Illustrated*.  55:11 Ap 99

---

**Periodical Call Slip**

Magazine (Periodical) Article _____

Author (s) _____

Periodical Title _____

Volume _____         Page (s) _____

Month _____         Year _____

Your Name _____

Hand this call slip to your librarian so that he or she can find the magazine article for you.

---

# Standards

Students will

- Use the *Readers' Guide to Periodical Literature* and other indexes to gather information (McREL 5)

- Access information efficiently and accurately (AASL/AECT 1)

- Participate effectively in groups to pursue and generate information (AASL/AECT 9)

# Objectives

Students discuss the *Readers' Guide to Periodical Literature*. The class completes a *Readers' Guide* overhead transparency sheet. Student pairs fill out call slips from actual *Readers' Guide to Periodical Literature* entries.

# Directions

1. The *Readers' Guide* worksheet should be duplicated onto a transparency. To introduce the *Readers' Guide,* the class completes the transparency in language arts or library class.

2. The call slip sheet from the bottom of the worksheet should be copied for library class students.

3. In library class, the teacher explains that the *Readers' Guide to Periodical Literature* is a way to find a magazine article on any subject. Students should understand that the researching skills they will learn may be transferred to other resources.

4. The teacher tells students that magazines are called periodicals. (Perhaps the class could brainstorm a list of periodicals that could be found in the *Readers' Guide.*) Then students are told that periodical titles are in italicized print, and that subjects are in bold capitalized letters. Although they all look alike, almost every *Readers' Guide to Periodical Literature* contains different magazine or periodical articles.

5. Student pairs will practice filling out a "Periodical Call Slip" from an actual *Readers' Guide to Periodical Literature.* They can choose any subject. To save time, students may be given a broad topic, such as sports. If possible, students may also be given their desired magazine articles from their call slips.

6. At a later time, students should practice filling out call slips once more. As students learn how to fill out call slips, they should also learn how to use CD-ROM magazine indexes, such as *MAS* or *INFOTRAC.*

# Learning Styles

Linguistic (reading and writing) and interpersonal (group work)

# Teaching Team

Language arts and library teachers

# Suggested Resources

*INFOTRAC.* Foster City, CA: Information Access Company, 1998 [CD-ROM].

*MAS.* Ipsovich, MA: EBSCO Publishing, 2001 [CD-ROM].

*Readers' Guide to Periodical Literature.* New York: H. W. Wilson, 2001.

# Once Upon a Time . . .

Fairy tale elements can include the following:
- Characters can be many different things, including fairies, elves, goblins, kings and queens.
- The theme can be magic.
- Fairy tales may begin with the phrase, "Once upon a time..." It may end with the phrase, "They lived happily ever after."
- Characters are usually either very good or very bad.

Answer the following questions after reading a fairy tale:

1. What is the title? _____

2. Where is the geographic location (setting)? _____

_____

3. List and then briefly describe the main characters:

_____

_____

_____

_____

4. Explain the main plot in one sentence: _____

_____

5. Now look back at what you have written for setting, plot, and characters. Rewrite the fairy tale to make it happen today. Use the back of this sheet to write a new, but short fairy tale.

## Standards

Students will

- Understand the defining features and structures of fantasies, fables, and fairy tales at this developmental level (McREL 17)
- Appreciate literature and other creative expressions (AASL/AECT 5)
- Participate effectively in groups to pursue and generate information (AASL/AECT 9)

## Objectives

Students review fairy tale elements. Student groups read fairy tale books or view fairy tale CD-ROMs. Student groups write down the title, geographic location, main characters, and plot from their fairy tales on worksheets. Student groups create fractured fairy tales.

## Directions

1. The library teacher provides students with the fairy tale worksheet.
2. The teacher briefly reviews some elements of fairy tales from the worksheet.
3. The teacher points out the location of fairy tale books on the shelf and on CD-ROM. (Some popular fairy tale CD-ROMs are the *Talking Classic Tales* or *The Greatest Children's Stories Ever Told*.)
4. Student groups choose and then read a fairy tale from a book or CD-ROM.
5. As groups answer their worksheet questions, they will find ideas for their own creative fairy tales or fractured fairy tales.
6. Students should keep the stories fairly short in the interest of time. Students may write their stories on the backs of their worksheets or compose the stories on computers during the library or language arts class.
7. Students may share their stories during language arts class. The language arts teacher may wish to have students turn their stories into animated versions using the *Castle* CD-ROM or *Ultimate Writing and Creativity Center* CD-ROM.

## Learning Styles

Interpersonal (group work), linguistic (reading, writing, and telling stories), spatial (creating), and mathematical (computers)

## Teaching Team

Language arts and library teachers

## Suggested Resources

Any fairy tale book.

*Castle.* Novato, CA: The Learning Company, 1998 [CD-ROM].

*Greatest Stories Ever Told.* New York: New Media Schoolhouse, 1983 [CD-ROM].

*Talking Classic Tales.* Pound Ridge, NY: New Media Schoolhouse, 1991 [CD-ROM].

*Ultimate Writing and Creativity Center.* Novato, CA: The Learning Company, 2000 [CD-ROM].

# Name That President!

\*\*\*\*\*\*\*\*\*\*\*\*\*\*\*\*\*\*\*\*\*\*\*\*\*\*\*\*\*\*\*\*\*\*\*\*\*\*\*\*\*\*\*\*\*\*\*\*\*\*\*\*\*\*

1. This is what this president said (from the quotation book):

_____

_____


2. These are two things he did (from the biographical dictionary):

1. _____

_____

2. _____

_____

3. Which president was he (from biographical dictionary)? Number ___

## Standards

Students will

- Understand the defining features and structure of biographies and autobiographies at this developmental level (McREL 20)
- Demonstrate a familiarity with a variety of selected nonfiction (McREL 23)
- Access information efficiently and effectively (AASL/AECT 1)
- Evaluate information critically and competently (AASL/AECT 2)
- Use information accurately and creatively (AASL/AECT 3)
- Pursue information related to personal interest (AASL/AECT 4)
- Recognize the importance of information to a democratic society (AASL/AECT 7)

## Objectives

Students will learn how to use quotation books and biographical dictionaries. Student pairs will choose a president and then find a quote by that president using the quotation book and locate facts about him from the biographical dictionary.

## Directions

1. The library teacher locates three or more copies of quotation books and biographical dictionaries for this activity. The teacher shows students how to use these resources before the activity begins.

2. Student pairs will choose a president, different from the others.

3. Student pairs will need to use a quotation book and the biographical dictionary to answer their worksheets. They will find a quotation by their president and then some facts about him from the biographical dictionary.

4. In social studies class, students create a guessing game about their chosen president. Once students have completed presidential worksheets, the social studies class tries to guess the president from each student worksheet. If desired, the worksheets can be cut along the line in order to have the questions stapled to the top half of the sheet to create a guessing game. For a follow-up, social studies students could find out more about presidents by using the *Portraits of American Presidents* CD-ROM.

## Learning Styles

Linguistic (reading and writing) and mathematical (challenging games)

## Teaching Team

Library and social studies teachers

## Suggested Resources

Bartlett, John. *Bartlett's Familiar Quotations*. Boston: Little, Brown, 1992.

*Merriam Webster's Biographical Dictionary*. Springfield, MA: Merriam Webster, 1995.

*Portraits of American Presidents*. Salt Lake City, UT: Questar, 1995 [CD-ROM].

# Information Please

The almanac contains more than one million pieces of information. It is published every year with even more facts. Did you know that the index is in the front of an almanac?

Look up the following facts in the *Information Please Almanac*:

1. How much does the Statue of Liberty weigh? _____

2. What is the population of the country of Peru? _____

3. Which country has the most computers? _____

4. What team won the Orange Bowl (college football) game in 1979?

_____

5. Who won the 1992 Winter Olympic gold medal for women's figure skating? _____

6. Who discovered the planet Uranus? _____

7. Where was the 1965 tornado disaster in the United States?

_____

8. How much money does the U.S. president make? (Look under United States government.) _____

# Standards

Students will

- Use multiple representations of information (e.g., maps, charts) to find information for research purposes (McREL 4)
- Use key words, indexes, cross references, and letters on volumes to find information for research purposes (McREL 3)
- Access information efficiently and effectively (AASL/AECT 1)
- Evaluate information critically and competently (AASL/AECT 2)
- Use information accurately and creatively (AASL/AECT 3)
- Pursue information related to personal interest (AASL/AECT 4)
- Participate effectively in groups to pursue and generate information (AASL/AECT 9)

# Objectives

Students discuss the purpose of almanacs. Students grasp how to use almanacs. Student groups search almanacs to answer questions on the worksheets.

# Directions

1. Students receive the almanac worksheets. They will find answers to the worksheet questions in the *Information Please Almanac*. Students need access to several copies of the *Information Please Almanac*. (*The World Almanac* will also work.)

2. The library teacher explains that the purpose of almanacs is to provide quick facts on a million or more things. The teacher explains that the index is located in front of some almanacs, including the *Information Please Almanac*.

3. Before beginning their searches, the teacher will remind students how to find key words and how to locate topics.

4. Group students according to the number of the available almanacs.

5. Student groups will find as many worksheet answers as possible. This activity can be timed. This activity can also be set up as a competition game between groups.

6. If students complete their worksheets early, they can browse through almanacs to find some interesting facts to share with the class. The class could also look at *Information Please* online.

7. For an almanac follow-up, the social studies teacher may have students locate information regarding different states in the almanac.

# Learning Styles

Linguistic (reading), mathematical (playing challenging games), interpersonal (group work), and spatial (reading charts)

# Teaching Team

Library and social studies teachers

## Suggested Resources

Famighetti, Robert, editor. *World Almanac and Book of Facts*. Mahwah, NJ: World Almanac, 2001.

Johnson, Otto, Editor. *Information Please Almanac*. Boston: Houghton Mifflin, 2000.

# Macbeth

Shakespeare wrote a play called *Macbeth*. Read or listen to the Macbeth picture-book story. Now answer these questions about the story.

**Part 1: Three Scary Creatures in the Misty Night**
What did the three creatures in the misty night tell Macbeth at the very start of the story?
Did Macbeth believe what the creatures said?

**Part 2: Macbeth and the Lady Macbeth Have an Evil Plan**
Why did Lady Macbeth want to hurt the king?
What was the evil plan of Lady Macbeth?

**Part 3: Macduff Doubts Macbeth**
Why did Macduff doubt Macbeth?

**Part 4: The Banquet**
What did Macbeth see at the banquet? Was it real?

**Part 5: The Final Battle**
How does the story of Macbeth end?

**Your Thoughts:** What can be learned from the story? What is the moral?

## Standards

Students will

- Demonstrate a basic familiarity with a variety of selected classic fiction, folktales, and poetry (McREL 22)

- Appreciate literature and other creative expressions (AASL/AECT 5)

## Objectives

Students listen to and then discuss a version of *Macbeth*. Student groups will describe and write down the story parts.

## Directions

1. The library teacher provides students with copies of the Macbeth worksheet.

2. The teacher reads the Shakespearean picture book of *Macbeth* (illustrated by Eric Kincaid) or has students view the video format of *Macbeth*. The teacher pauses once in a while to discuss what has happened in the story.

3. After reading the story, the teacher will put the main character's names of Macbeth, Lady Macbeth, and Macduff on the board, in order that the class may list the actions of the characters.

4. Students will form small groups to answer the worksheet questions.

5. As a follow-up, students may act out the story in language arts class.

## Learning Styles

Linguistic (writing) and bodily kinesthetic (acting)

## Teaching Team

Language arts and library teachers

## Suggested Resources

Kincaid, Eric. *William Shakespeare's Macbeth*. New Market, England: Brimax Books, 1997.

*Macbeth* (Animated Shakespeare Series). United Kingdom: BBC Publications, 1992 [video].

## What's It All About?

What's this book all about?  These text helpers help you find out about things in nonfiction books: the chapter headings, topic sentences, and the summary sentences.

Find a nonfiction book. Then use the text helpers in the first chapter:

1.  What is the heading (title) of chapter one? _____

_____

2.  Find the topic sentence in the first paragraph.  What is your paragraph's topic? (The topic sentence tells what the paragraph is all about in one sentence.) _____

_____

3.  Find the topic sentence in the second paragraph. _____

_____

4.  Find a summary sentence in the first section. (The summary sentence will tell what the whole section is all about in one sentence.) Paraphrase or explain it in your own words. _____

_____

_____

## Standards

Students will

- Use chapter and section headings, topic sentences, and summary sentences to construct the main idea (McREL 15)

- Access information efficiently and effectively (AASL/AECT 1)

- Strive for excellence in information seeking (AASL/AECT 6)

## Objectives

Students locate the main idea of a paragraph by using headings, topic sentences, and summary sentences in nonfiction books. Students first locate the main idea as a group and then individually.

## Directions

1. This lesson teaches students how to locate the main idea in nonfiction books. Students will use either nonfiction books or their textbooks.

2. The library teacher makes an overhead transparency and student copies of the worksheet. The class will first answer the overhead sheets as a whole group and then individually.

3. The library teacher should also make a transparency of a short chapter from a nonfiction book for whole-class viewing.

4. To create whole-class understanding, the teacher will read the paragraph from the overhead sheet, and then the class will answer the transparency worksheet questions.

5. Once the class understands the use of text helpers such as the heading, topic sentence, and summary sentence, individual students will answer the worksheet questions using a nonfiction book or textbook.

6. In social studies or science class, students may locate the main idea in their textbook to reinforce main idea.

## Learning Styles

Linguistic (reading and writing), interpersonal (group work), and intrapersonal (working alone)

## Teaching Team

Library, science, and social studies teachers

## Suggested Resources

Social studies or science textbooks and other nonfiction sources.

# Sailing the World Web

URL (Internet address): http://_____

Describe the site: _____

_____

Read some of the information on the site.  Then check yes or no:

| Criteria | Yes | No |
| --- | --- | --- |
| 1. Easy to find things? | | |
| 2. Like the pictures? | | |
| 3. Is the author's name given? | | |
| 4. Teachers will use it?<br>   Students will use it? | | |
| 5. Does it have facts? | | |

------------------------

6. Explain why you think (or don't think) that this is good Internet site for your school to use.

_____

_____

_____

7. Download a terrific picture from the Internet site.  Circle the URL on the printout.

Bonus:  Does the site have a date?  What is it? _____

## Standards

Students will

- Understand the concept of "likely informant" for obtaining information about a specific topic (McREL 9)

- Access information efficiently and effectively (AASL/AECT 1)

- Evaluate information critically and competently (AASL/AECT 2)

- Recognize the importance of information to a democratic society (AASL/AECT 7)

- Practice ethical behavior in regard to information and information technology (AASL/AECT 8)

## Objectives

Students learn how to recognize good Internet sites. Student pairs will evaluate Web sites.

## Directions

1. Fifth-grade students will realize the potential of information resources located on the Internet. Students should also be aware that some Internet sites may not always contain accurate information.

2. The library teacher and the technologist will show students how to compose rudimentary Internet searches to obtain information. Students should be told that the letters URL represent the Internet address. The teachers provide students with some approved Internet addresses like the following:

   http://www.infomall.org/kidsweb (Information on all subjects for children)

   http://www.yaholigans.com (Information on all subjects for children)

   http://www.eb.com (Encyclopedia Britannia)

   http://www.biography.com (Biographies)

   http:/nationalgeographic.com (Science, animals, and so on just for children)

3. The teacher gives student pairs time to browse the Web sites.

4. Paired students learn to evaluate Internet sites for accuracy while using the Internet worksheet. Students evaluate one or two Internet sites.

5. For a follow-up, language arts students may research some Internet topics from a teacher-approved list.

## Learning Styles

Mathematical (using computers), linguistic (reading), and interpersonal (working with others)

## Teaching Team

Language arts, library, and technology teachers

## Suggested Resources

The computer lab.

# Myths Flow Like the Rivers of Truth

 Long ago, storytellers used mystical creatures as a way to explain the ways of nature.  These beliefs became myths, traditional stories that explain a world view.  Myths came from many cultures, including the Greek, Chinese, Mexican, Native American, Norse, and from other peoples.

Directions:  Read a Native American myth. Then complete the blanks to construct a teepee, the dwelling of certain early North American tribes.

Mythology Tepee

of the _____

(title)

1. _____

2. _____, _____

3. _____, _____, _____

4. _____, _____, _____, _____

5. _____, _____, _____, _____, _____

1. Name one main character.
2. Write two words to describe the main character.
3. In three words describe the setting.
4. List four other characters.
5. Finally describe the plot in five words.

## Standards

Students will

- Understand the defining features and structures of myths at this developmental level (McREL 19)

- Appreciate literature and other creative expressions (AASL/AECT 5)

- Practice ethical behavior in regard to information an information technology (AASL/AECT 8)

## Objectives

Students summarize myths. Small student groups will read a Native American myth. Students will describe plot, setting, and characters from their myth.

## Directions

1. The library teacher asks students to explain what they recall about myths. Then the teacher summarizes those explanations.

2. Next, small groups of students read a Native American myth. (Examples of easy-reading Native American myths are Paul Goble's tales: *Buffalo Women*, *Iktomi and the Coyote*, or *Remaking the Earth: A Creation Story*.)

3. After reading the myth, students fill in the blanks on their myth worksheets to describe the characters, setting, and plot. After filling in the blanks, students see the form of a teepee, as seen in the Goble books.

4. Students share their worksheet responses with the class.

5. Social studies students may research different early Native American tribes to uncover their lifestyles. Students may use the *Native Americans* CD-ROM or other sources.

## Learning Styles

Linguistic (reading and writing), interpersonal (group work), and intrapersonal (working alone)

## Teaching Team

Library and social studies teachers

## Suggested Resources

Goble, Paul. *Buffalo Women*. New York: Bradbury Press, 1984.

Goble, Paul. *Iktomi and the Coyote*. New York: Orchard Books, 1998.

Goble, Paul. *Remaking the Earth: A Creation Story*. New York: Orchard Books, 1996.

*Native Americans*. Raleigh, NC: Rainbow Educational Media, 1998 [CD-ROM].

# Newbery Book Review

After reading a Newbery book, you will need to complete the following:

I. Your Newbery book title: _____

   Author: _____

II. What is the genre of your fiction book?  Circle the genre:
Historical Fiction, Mystery, Humorous, Science Fiction, Animal, Realistic

III.  Think of a setting for your Newbery book.  Then show it by presenting
<u>one</u> of these activities to your class:
    1. Illustrate the setting with a diorama using small lifelike objects.
    2. Act out a scene in front of a poster-sized background of the setting.
    3. Recite a poem or sing a song about the setting of the book.

IV. Explain the main plot of your book in one paragraph.

_____

_____

_____

_____

_____

V.  How would you describe the theme of the book? Write 1 or 2 sentences.

_____

_____

_____

VI.  List the main characters and define them very briefly.

_____

_____

_____

_____

_____

VII. What is your opinion? Would you tell someone to read this Newbery
book? Why or why not?

_____

_____

_____

Did you do well? Your teacher will fill in your rubric when you hand this in.
-------------------------------------------------------------------------------
 Newbery Rubric   (completed by your teacher)

| Activity | Not Yet | OK | Quality (Shows Effort) |
|---|---|---|---|
| Genre | 1 | 2 | 3 |
| Setting | 1 | 2 | 3 |
| Plot | 1 | 2 | 3 |
| Character | 1 | 2 | 3 |
| Theme | 1 | 2 | 3 |
| Your opinion | 1 | 2 | 3 |
| Neatly done | 1 | 2 | 3 |
| Correct spelling | 1 | 2 | 3 |

## Standards

Students will

- Explain how characters or simple events in a work are like people or events in one's own life (McREL 13)

- Recognize basic elements of plot (McREL 14)

- Become aware of the geographic information important to the story read (McREL 10)

- Understand the defining features and structures of mysteries, realistic fiction, historical fiction, adventure stories and humorous stories at this developmental level (McREL 18)

- Appreciate literature and other creative expressions (AASL/AECT 5)

## Objectives

Students discuss Newbery books. Students read a Newbery book and then describe plot, theme, and characters. Students will present setting.

## Directions

1. All students will read a Newbery Award or Newbery Honor book. The library teacher will make individual student copies of the Newbery worksheets.

2. The teacher gives a brief historical background of the Newbery award: John Newbery was acclaimed for having written the first children's books. Later, the American Library Association decided to give a yearly Newbery award for the best-written older children's book.

3. The library teacher book talks some Newbery books.

4. Students will find a Newbery book to read.

5. In library or language arts class, students answer worksheet questions on general story parts after reading their Newbery books. The language arts teacher should remind students that a theme is the lesson or the moral of the story, such as needing to belong or needing to accomplish something. Plot is what happens in the story. Setting is where the story takes place. Characters are the people or creatures in stories.

6. Students will illustrate, act out, or create a poem on the setting.

7. As a follow-up, students may view the Newbery book *Ralph S. Mouse* on videodisc or on videotape.

## Learning Styles

Linguistic (reading and writing), intrapersonal (working alone), spatial (art), musical (song or poem), and bodily kinesthetic (being active)

## Teaching Team

Language arts and library teachers

## Suggested Resources

George, Jean Craighead. *Julie of the Wolves*. New York: Harper & Row, 1972.

Lawson, Robert. *Rabbit Hill*. New York: Viking, 1944.

L'Engle, Madeline. *Wrinkle in Time*. New York: Ariel Books, 1962.

Levine, Gail Carson. *Ella Enchanted*. New York: HarperCollins, 1997.

Lowery, Lois. *Giver*. Boston: Houghton Mifflin, 1993.

Naylor, Phyllis Reynolds. *Shiloh*. New York: Atheneum, 1991.

*Ralph S. Mouse*. New York: Churchill, 1990 [video disc].

Raskin, Ellen. *Westing Game*. New York: Dutton, 1978.

Sperry, Armstrong. *Call It Courage*. New York: Macmillan, 1940.

Other Newbery titles can be found online at http://www.ala.org/alsc/newbery

# It's Against the Law!

It is against the law to copy copyrighted information. When you copy something word for word from another source, it is called plagiarism. Remember to always use your own words. Using your own words is called paraphrasing.

Directions: Practice paraphrasing! 1. Find an article in the encyclopedia. 2. Read the first paragraph. 3. Write down the most important information from the paragraph, without copying it word for word (paraphrase).

Your encyclopedia article:

_____

Read the first paragraph. Then paraphrase:

_____

_____

_____

_____

_____

_____

## Standards

Students will

- Use encyclopedias to gather information for research topics (McREL 1)
- Pursue information related to personal interest (AASL/AECT 4)
- Practice ethical behavior in regard to information and information technology (AASL/AECT 8)
- Participate effectively in groups to pursue and generate information (AASL/AECT 9)

## Objectives

Students discuss paraphrasing and copyright. Working as a class, students paraphrase two or three brief sentences. Student pairs paraphrase a brief encyclopedia paragraph.

## Directions

1. The library teacher makes a transparency and student copies of the worksheet.
2. The library teacher explains plagiarism since some students have difficulty expressing their own thoughts or paraphrasing.
3. While viewing the transparency, students will try paraphrasing as a whole group, as the teacher reads two or three short sentences from any informational source. (This activity may need to be repeated.)
4. When the teacher feels that the class knows how to paraphrase, student pairs can begin working. Student pairs will need to find an encyclopedia article in either print or electronic version. They will need to read the first paragraph in their chosen article. Finally, they will paraphrase their information on their worksheets.
5. To reinforce paraphrasing, students should paraphrase a paragraph from another encyclopedia or nonfiction source in language arts class.

## Learning Styles

Linguistic (reading and writing) and interpersonal (group work)

## Teaching Team

Language arts and library teachers

## Suggested Resources

*Encyclopedia Britannica*. Chicago: Britannica, 2001 [CD-ROM].

*Microsoft Encarta Encyclopedia Deluxe 2001*. Richmond, WA: Microsoft, 2001 [CD-ROM].

*World Book 2001 Multimedia Deluxe*. Chicago: World Book, 2001 [CD-ROM].

*World Book Encyclopedia*. Chicago: 2001 [CD-ROM].

# Which Reference Is It?

Cut out these cards. Write the answers on the back. Then have someone guess the answer.

---

**Which reference is it?**

Q. This reference tells what words mean. Which reference is it?

---

**Which reference is it?**

Q. This reference tells words that mean the same. Which reference is it?

---

**Which reference is it?**

Q. This reference tells what a famous person said. Which reference is it?

---

**Which reference is it?**

Q. This reference has a lot of maps. Which reference is it?

---

**Which reference is it?**

Q. This reference has information about a person, place, or thing. Which reference is it?

---

**Which reference is it?**

Q. This reference only gives quick facts. Which reference is it?

---

**Which reference is it?**

Q. This reference helps you find a magazine article. Which reference is it?

---

**Which reference is it?**

Q. This reference has general information about geographic places. Which reference is it?

## Standards

Students will

- Demonstrate a familiarity with a variety of selected nonfiction (McREL 23)
- Strive for excellence in information seeking (AASL/AECT 6)

## Objectives

Students define and review reference sources. Students create a reference game quiz. Students quiz each other on reference sources.

## Directions

1. The library teacher reviews some basic facts about these references: Almanacs (gives quick facts), atlas (includes maps), quotation books (tells what famous people say), geographic dictionary (gives general information about towns, rivers, etc.), encyclopedia (has information about a person, place, or thing), thesaurus (shows words that mean the same), dictionary (has definitions of words), and the *Readers' Guide to Periodical Literature* (tells where to find magazine articles on certain things). The teacher lists the titles of those sources on the board.

2. Following the review, students quiz each other. They will cut out the worksheet game cards and then write the correct answers on the backs of the cards. (The teacher lists the answers on the board.) Students work in small groups to quiz each other with the reference game cards, giving everyone a chance to be the game host.

3. If the library teacher would rather have students take a reference quiz than do a game, the questions may be asked orally. Students will write down the correct answers on a blank sheet.

4. Once the groups are finished with the game or quiz, they will browse through those listed references, looking at not only print versions, but at CD-ROM references (such as *Infopedia*, *Microsoft Encarta*, or the *World Book Multimedia*).

5. For a follow-up, the language arts teacher may have students use those references for a research project.

## Learning Styles

Linguistic (writing and reading)

## Teaching Team

Language arts and library teachers

## Suggested Resources

Bartlett, John. *Bartlett's Familiar Quotations*. Boston: Little, Brown, 1992.

*Infopedia*. Richmond, WA: Softkey/Microsoft, 2000 [CD-ROM].

*Merriam Webster's Geographic Dictionary*. Springfield, MA: Merriam Webster, 1997.

*Microsoft Encarta Encyclopedia Deluxe 2001*. Richmond, WA: Microsoft, 2001 [CD-ROM].

*Readers' Guide to Periodical Literature*. New York: H. W. Wilson, 2001.

*World Almanac, 2001*. Mahwah, NJ: World Almanac, 2001.

*World Book 2001 Multimedia Deluxe*. Chicago: World Book, 2001 [CD-ROM].

# Keying in to Research

I. Explain your research project.
1. What is the topic of your research paper?_____
2. When is your research paper due? _____
3. What is the required length of your research paper? _____

II. Brainstorm
List the titles of resources that you might use:
1. _____
2. _____
3. _____
4. _____
5. _____

III. Provide a bibliography of resources that you will use:
1. Author of the book: _____
   Title of the book: _____
   Copyright: _____ Publisher: _____
   Publishing place: _____
   Page (s): _____

2. Author of the magazine article: _____
   Magazine (Periodical) title: _____
   Month, day, and year of the magazine: _____
   Page (s): _____

3. Encyclopedia article: _____
   Encyclopedia title: _____
   Copyright: _____ Circle if this was a CD-ROM.

IV. Note time

1. Circle how you will record the information that you found:
   Note cards              Word processor           Tape player
2. Go ahead and start taking notes!

V. Type your paper

1. Use the word processor.
2. Check your spelling on the computer.
3. Double space after all periods.
4. Have a title.

VI. How did you do?

1. Did you spend enough time?     Yes     No     Maybe
2. Were you neat?     Yes     No     Maybe
3. Did you follow all steps?     Yes     No     Maybe
4. Did you do well?     Yes     No     Maybe

## Standards

Students will

- Use encyclopedias to gather information for research topic (McREL 1)

- Use the *Readers' Guide to Periodical Literature* and other indexes to gather information (McREL 5)

- Use a computer catalog to gather information for research purposes (McREL 7)

- Gather information for research topics using note taking (McREL 8)

- Demonstrate a basic competence in using a variety of selected nonfiction (McREL 23)

- Access information efficiently and effectively (AASL/AECT 1)

- Evaluate information critically and competently (AASL/AECT 2)

- Use information accurately and creatively (AASL/AECT 3)

- Strive for excellence in information seeking (ASL/AECT 6)

## Objectives

Students brainstorm research topics. Students research chosen topics. Students create bibliographies. Students take notes and then type a two-paragraph paper. Students complete their own self-evaluations.

## Directions

1.  The library teacher gives students a topic to research, such as an invention.

2.  The teacher provides students with the research worksheet. The language arts or library teacher tells the class when their paper is due and how long their research paper will be. One to two paragraphs may be enough.

3.  Students should use the following sources: a nonfiction book (when found on the automated card catalog), a magazine article (located on *INFOTRAC* or *MAS* CD-ROM or in the *Readers' Guide to Periodical Literature*), and an encyclopedia article (found on CD-ROM, like *Microsoft Encarta* or *World Book 2001 Multimedia Deluxe*, on Internet such as *Encyclopedia Britannica*'s http://www.eb.com, or in any print volume).

4.  Next students locate their resources. Once resources are found, students fill out the bibliographic formats with the assistance of the library teacher.

5.  In language arts class, students start taking notes. Students neatly copy down notes or highlight printed copies from sources.

6.  In language arts or library class, students will compile their notes into a final two-paragraph paper. They will use word processors to type their paragraphs. After completing their paragraphs, students will need to fill out their self-evaluations on their worksheets.

## Learning Styles

Linguistic (reading and writing), intrapersonal (work alone), and mathematical (computers)

## Teaching Team

Language arts and library teachers

## Suggested Resources

Any encyclopedias.

*http://www.eb.com* (Encyclopedia Britannica)

*INFOTRAC.* California: Information Access Company, 1998 [CD-ROM].

*MAS.* Ipsovich, MA: EBSCO Publishing, 2001 [CD-ROM].

*Microsoft Encarta Encyclopedia Deluxe 2001.* Richmond, WA: Microsoft, 2001 [CD-ROM].

*Readers' Guide to Periodical Literature.* New York: H. W. Wilson, 2001.

*World Book 2001 Multimedia Deluxe.* Chicago: World Book, 2001 [CD-ROM].

# Bibliography

American Association of School Librarians and Association for Educational Communications and Technology. 1998. *Information Literacy Standards for Student Learning*. Chicago: American Library Association.

American Library Association and Association for Educational Communications and Technology. 1998. *Information Power: Building Partnerships for Learning*. Chicago: American Library Association.

American Association of School Librarians and Association for Educational Communications and Technology. 1988. *Information Power: Guidelines for School Library Media Programs*. Chicago: American Library Association.

Baule, Steven. 1999. Executive summary. Information power: Building partnerships for learning. *Book Report* (November/December): p. 43.

Gardener, Howard. 1983. *Frames of Mind: Theory of Multiple Intelligences*. New York: Basic Books

Kendall, John S., and Robert J. Marzano. 2000. *Content Knowledge: A Compendium of Standards and Benchmarks for K–12 Education*, 3rd ed. Aurora, CO: McREL.

Kovalik, Susan. 1994. *ITI: The Model. Integrated Thematic Instruction*. Kent, WA: Books for Educators, pp. 56–66. (Gardener)

Morris, Betty, John T. Gillespie, and Diana L. Spirt. 1992. *Administering the School Library Media Center*. New Providence, NJ: R. R. Bowker.

# Index